JIM'S JOURNEY
THROUGH THE BIBLE
— BOOK II —

By Jim Binns
Edited by Gary Ray

Disclaimer: Copyright © 2025 by Jim Binns. All rights reserved. You may quote and use up to 3,000 words for non-commercial personal use without prior permission from Covenant Press. Commercial use requires proper bibliographic attribution and is limited to 1,000 words without prior permission. Any use beyond these limitations must be approved by Covenant Press.

Covenant Press — New York, New York — ISBN: 978-1-954419-26-1

The journey of a thousand miles begins with a single step.

—𝔍𝔦𝔪 𝔅𝔦𝔫𝔫𝔰

Introduction

The journey of a thousand miles begins with a single step . . .

In Book II of *Jim's Journey Through the Bible* readers embark on an enlightening exploration that intertwines history, scripture, and significant biblical locations. This volume is not just a collection of stories; it's a rich tapestry of faith and human experience that brings to life the incredible journey of early Christians and the trials they faced.

As the narrative unfolds, the book delves deeply into various topics, shedding light on the profound lessons embedded within the scriptures. Each chapter carefully examines key figures and events, highlighting their relevance to contemporary life. From Abraham's steadfast faith and Moses' struggles to David's valor and Daniel's prophetic insights, every story is woven together to illustrate the powerful dynamics of faith, obedience, and divine intervention.

Moreover, this journey doesn't shy away from the darker elements of our existence. It addresses the chaos that Satan often creates, reminding readers that the battle between good and evil has been a powerful force throughout history. With a focus on God's sovereign love and grace, the book encourages readers to draw strength from these biblical narratives, offering insight and encouragement for their personal journeys.

"For the word of God is living and active, sharper than any two-edged sword, piercing to the division of soul and of spirit, of joints and of marrow, and discerning the thoughts and intentions of the heart."

—*Paul the Apostle* (Hebrews 4:12)

Table of Contents

NOAH AND THE GREAT FLOOD	5
ABRAHAM (ABRAM) AND HIS DESCENDANTS: CHRISTIANITY AND ISLAM	15
A LOOK AT THE BOOK OF JOB	21
THINGS YOU MAY NOT KNOW ABOUT MOSES	33
THE DISPUTE WITH SATAN OVER MOSES' BODY	52
THE LIFE AND TIMES OF JOSHUA	56
DAVID, THE KING OF ISRAEL	72
KING SOLOMON AND THE TEMPLES	101
THE STORY OF ELIJAH	115
THE BOOK OF DANIEL	122
THE BOOK OF EZEKIEL	148
TEMPLE HISTORY AND FUTURE	162
BABYLON	178
THE TWO WITNESSES	183
CHRISTIANITY AND ISLAM	185
ONCE SAVED, ALWAYS SAVED	196
CREDITS	205

Noah and The Great Flood

The story of Noah and the Great Flood has been told to many generations, but there is more to this story than most people realize. Allow me to introduce some of the players in this magnificent story.

God created the first male and female, naming them **Adam** and **Eve**. They had three sons: **Cain, Abel, and Seth**. Cain killed Abel; God cursed Cain, and Cain eventually settled in the land of Nod, east of Eden.

Adam lived a total of 930 years. **Seth** lived 912 years and was the father of **Enosh,** who lived 905 years and was the father of **Kenan** (also spelled Qenan, Kaynan, or Cainan). Then **Mahalalel** (ma-hal-a-lel) was born to Kenan, who died when he was 910. Mahalalel was the father of **Jared,** and Mahalalel lived a total of 895 years. Jared lived a total of 962 years and was the father of **Enoch** *and* **Methuselah**. (Enoch walked faithfully with God for 365 years, and then he was no more, because God took him away). Methuselah lived 969 years and was the oldest man listed in the Bible.

He was the father of **Lamech** (lay-mech), who lived 777 years, and had a son named **Noah.** When Noah was 500 years old, he became the father of **Shem,** then **Ham**, and then Japheth (ja-peth). Noah was six hundred years old when the flood of water came upon the earth (Genesis 7:6). For a timeline of Noah's family, look at Genesis 5-10.

God told Noah to build the ark because He planned to destroy all flesh with a great flood as judgment on sinners. God is holy, perfect, and pure, set apart from anything sinful.

> ***"And GOD saw that the wickedness of man was great in the earth, and that every imagination of the thoughts of his heart was only evil continually."***

When God looked down upon the beautiful world and saw all the sin and corruption *". . . it grieved him at his heart"* (Genesis 6:6).

The Ark: God said to Noah, "*Make for yourself an ark of gopher wood; you shall make the ark with rooms, and shall cover it inside and out with pitch. This is how you shall make it: the length of the ark three hundred cubits, its breadth fifty cubits, and its height thirty cubits. You shall make a window for the ark, and finish it to a cubit from the top; and set the door of the ark in the side of it; you shall make it with lower, second, and third decks.*"

The word "*ark*" in Hebrew is "*tebah*," meaning a large vessel or container. *Pitch* is a black, sticky waterproofing material that can be made from pine trees. The size of the ark is staggering. Three hundred cubits (450 feet), 50 cubits (75 feet), and thirty cubits (45 feet). (The average football field is 360 feet long.) This equals roughly 1,518,750 cubic feet aboard and is comparable to 569 modern railroad boxcars.

Today, a cubit is equal to 1.5 feet. But the cubit, as an ancient unit of measurement, was the length of the forearm from the elbow to the most extended finger. The ancient Egyptian royal cubit is known to have been approximately 20 to 22 inches.

So, doing the math using the Egyptian royal cubit—the ark could have been up to 550 feet long, 91.7 feet wide, and 55 feet high (1,856,250 cubic feet). The ark had three levels with many rooms (Genesis 6:14). God also told Noah to store portions of every food, enough for his family and the animals.

Noah was instructed to build the ark of **gofer**, a word not otherwise used in the Bible or the Hebrew language. The exact type of wood is unknown, but some scholars suggest that gofer (gopher wood) might have been cypress, pine, or another resinous tree (Genesis 6:14).

The Bible does not explicitly say how long Noah took to build the ark. However, a few Bible statements would help make a reasonable estimate of how long the process took. After Noah was 500 years old, he became the father of Shem, Ham, and Japheth (Genesis 5:32). Noah received the command to build the ark in (Genesis 6:14). By the time Noah entered the ark, and the flood began, Noah was 600 years old (Genesis 7:6).

Based on these statements, the time it took to build the ark could be about 100 years; however, some scholars believe it took Noah 120 years. Regardless of Noah's time, completing the ark could not have been easy.

Animals on the Ark: Most people think that Noah took two of every kind of animal into the ark, but that is not what happened. The Bible states, *"Take with you seven pairs of every kind of clean animal, a male and its mate, and one pair of every kind of unclean animal, a male and its mate, and also seven pairs of every kind of bird, male and female, to keep their various kinds alive throughout the earth"* (Genesis 7:2–3).

Though it is not known precisely what is meant by a biblical "kind," dogs are generally considered to be fertile animals within their groups. Dogs can breed with any dog; therefore, dogs are one kind. Representatives from each type would only be necessary since the parents could have offspring carrying genetic information for all variations within their kind.

> *"Then Noah built an altar to the Lord and, taking some of all the clean animals and clean birds, he sacrificed burnt offerings on it"* (Genesis 8:20).

Since seven pairs of every clean animal were aboard, even after sacrifices were made there would still have left plenty of animals to begin replenishing the earth.

Clean and Unclean: Later in the Old Testament Book of Leviticus (11), God told Moses and Aaron which animals the Israelites could and could not eat.

"Of all the animals that live on land, these are the ones you may eat: You may eat any animal with a divided hoof and that chews the cud. Of all the creatures living in the water of the seas and the streams you may eat any that have fins and scales."

Some clean animals include cattle, deer, goats, sheep, seafood with fins and scales, certain birds, including chickens, doves, and ducks, and even some insects, such as grasshoppers and locusts.

Some of the unclean animals include pigs, dogs, cats, horses, donkeys, and rats, seafood lacking either fins or scales, such as shellfish, lobster, oysters, and catfish, some birds, such as owls, hawks, and vultures, and other animals, such as reptiles and amphibians.

The New Testament teaches that we are no longer judged about what foods we eat (Colossians 2:16). Keep in mind that we see the Leviticus list of clean and unclean animals much later than the timeframe of Noah and the flood.

The Flood: Noah and his family (8 people) had found grace in the eyes of God. **Noah, his wife, sons, Shem, Ham, Japheth, and their wives** entered the ark. And on the 600th year of Noah's life, on the 17th day of the 2nd month—on that day, all the springs of the great deep burst forth, and the floodgates of the heavens were opened.

"And it came to pass after seven days, that the waters of the flood were upon the earth. And rain fell on the earth forty days and forty nights" (Genesis 7:11).

The flood was on the earth *for forty days and forty nights, and the water lifted the ark and* moved about on the surface. All the high hills under the whole heaven were covered. And all flesh died that moved on the earth: birds and cattle and beasts and every creeping thing that creeps on the earth, and every man. Only Noah and those who were with him in the ark remained alive. The water was on the world for 150 days (almost five months).

Then God made a wind pass over the earth, and at the end of 150 days, the water had subsided, and the ark came to rest on the mountains of Ararat. The waters continued to recede, and after forty days, Noah opened a window he had made in the ark and sent out a raven and then a dove to see if they could find a place to perch. But they found no dry land and returned to the ark.

Noah waited seven more days and sent out the dove from the ark again. When the dove returned to him in the evening, a freshly plucked olive leaf was in its beak. He waited seven more days and sent the dove out again, but it did not return to him this time.

"By the first day of the first month of Noah's six hundred and first year, the water had dried up from the earth. Noah then removed the covering from the ark and saw that the surface of the ground was dry. By the twenty-seventh day of the second month the earth was completely dry."

Noah and his family leave the ark: God then tells Noah and his family to come out of the ark and bring all the living creatures with them so they can multiply on the earth. Noah then built an altar for the Lord, and with some of the clean animals and birds, he sacrificed burnt offerings. The Lord smelled the pleasing aroma and said, "Never again will I curse the ground because of humans, even though every inclination of the human heart is evil from childhood. And never again will I destroy all living creatures, as I have done."

God then blessed Noah and his sons and told them to be fruitful, increase in number, and fill the earth. God gave them dominion over all the beasts of the earth, birds in the sky, every creature that moves along the ground, and on all the fish in the sea. *"Everything that lives and moves about will be food for you, and just as I gave you the green plants, I now give you everything."*

Meat and Lifeblood: Noah and his family were now allowed to kill animals for food, but God told them not to eat meat that has its lifeblood still in it (Genesis 9). There are several suggested reasons that in the Old Testament, God prohibited the consumption of animal blood. One was to teach respect for the sacredness of life.

Blood is viewed as a symbol of life throughout the Bible, and the shedding of blood represents the loss of life. In the New Testament, the *"blood of Christ"* is a familiar figure of speech for the *"death of Christ"* (Ephesians 2:13; 1 Peter 1:19). The early church urged Gentile believers to abstain from eating bloody meat not to offend their Jewish brothers and to distance themselves from the practices of the pagans (Acts 15:20).

Perhaps another reason for God's command not to eat bloody meat concerned the sacrifices. At this time, blood was used as the only atonement for sin so it was seen as a sacred thing (2 Chronicles 29:24; Hebrews 9:22).

And perhaps God did not want mankind to act like the carnivorous animals, who caught their prey and began eating it immediately. Instead, they were to drain the blood from the carcass and thus ensure the animal was dead before it was consumed. And even further, some have suggested God may have given this command for health reasons. Blood in meat means it is not fully cooked, and eating uncooked meat can lead to disease or sickness.

The Noahic Covenant: God established this covenant with Noah and his sons (Gen 8:20; 9:3-18). The covenant reinstates God's authority over man and man's responsibilities as stated in the Adamic Covenant and adds new responsibilities such as the relationship of man and the animal kingdom, eating animal flesh, draining blood before eating meat, establishing the death penalty, and being fruitful and multiplying on the earth.

The Bible says that God caused a **rainbow** to appear in the sky on that day and used it to promise Noah and all of mankind that He would never again destroy the earth and all its inhabitants in a worldwide flood. Neither mankind's wickedness nor righteousness affects this <u>unconditional</u> covenant.

This does not mean that God will never again destroy the earth, because He has promised to one day destroy the world by fire (2 Peter 3:10). The lesson to us is that when we see a rainbow, we should constantly be reminded of God's faithfulness and His amazing grace.

> *"God is patient toward you, not wishing that any should perish, but that all should reach repentance"* (2 Pet. 2:9).

At some point after the flood, Noah planted a vineyard that produced wine, and then he became drunk, passed out, and was found naked inside his tent. One of his three sons, Ham, walks into Noah's tent, sees his father naked, leaves the tent, and tells his brothers (Shem and Japheth) what He had seen. Instead of acting disrespectfully like Ham, they took a garment, walked backward to cover their father, and avoided seeing him naked. When Noah awoke from his wine and discovered what Ham had done, he said, "Cursed be Canaan! (Ham's son) The lowest of servants will he be to his brothers."

The statement "Cursed be Canaan" indicates a direct consequence of Ham's actions and reflects the nature of sin and its ramifications. It's important to note that the curse does not stop with Canaan but, interestingly, affects future generations. This verse is a gentle reminder of the necessity of vigilance and responsibility, especially in positions of influence or leadership. In this verse, we see a profound moment of consequence. Noah's drunkenness led to an embarrassing situation. It's also a powerful warning about how just one careless decision can destroy the reputation of even the godliest man or woman.

So, if you build something as big as this ark, you would think it would be easy to find after the flood. According to Genesis 8:4, the ark came to rest on the mountains of Ararat, a mountain range in Turkey.

"On the seventeenth day of the seventh month, the ark came to rest on the mountains of Ararat." This verse marks when Noah's ark found a resting place after the floodwaters receded, indicating a significant event in the Bible. The mountains of Ararat are traditionally associated with the location where the ark came to rest, symbolizing hope and new beginnings after the flood. Many expeditions have searched for the ark on Mount Ararat, while others have focused on nearby mountains in Iran. But no one has found it yet.

Noah was an obedient servant of God. He built an ark to preserve himself, his family, and representatives of every land animal from a great flood that God unleashed in judgment upon the earth. He was a man of great faith who believed in God's plan for salvation. After the flood, God blessed and made a covenant with him, sealing it with a rainbow.

Noah lived for 350 years after the flood and died at 950 years old (Genesis 9:28-29). This means he lived long enough to see the land restored after the flood and to see all three of his sons start their families and multiply.

Shem is considered the ancestor of the Semitic peoples, including the Hebrews and Arabs. Ham's descendants are often associated with Africa and parts of the Near East, and Japheth's lineage is traditionally linked to the peoples of Europe and parts of Asia.

Maranatha (*mar-a-na-tha*)
"Come Lord" or "Our Lord Come"

Other Questions:

The Canopy Theory: Obviously, early man's long life prior to the flood was much different from what we know today. Some scholars believe that this longer life was because the Earth's atmosphere may have had a "protective barrier" that restricted UV light and radiation from reaching the earth.

"And God said, Let there be a firmament in the midst of the waters, and let it divide the waters from the waters" (Genesis 1:6-9).

Some believe that before the flood this canopy of water "*firmament*" above the atmosphere created a greenhouse effect on the earth's climate and is thought to have provided torrential rains during the flood period. The first century historian Josephus however asserts man's longevity to God's mercy and the fact that the food they ate was much better at extending their years on earth than it was after the deluge.

Some people are skeptical that rain occurred on Earth before Noah's flood. Some interpret the scripture (Hebrews 11:7) as saying it had never rained before the Flood:

"By faith Noah, when warned about things not yet seen, in holy fear built an ark to save his family. By his faith he condemned the world and became heir of the righteousness that comes by faith."

Rain might be referred to as "things not yet seen," or it could be referring to the Flood in general.

Let's look at (Genesis 2:5-9):

"And every plant of the field before it was in the earth, and every herb of the field before it grew: for the LORD God had not caused it to rain upon the earth, and there was not a man to till the ground. But there went up a mist from the earth, and watered the whole face of the ground. Then the Lord God

formed the man of dust from the ground and breathed into his nostrils the breath of life, and the man became a living creature. And the Lord God planted a garden in Eden, in the east, and there he put the man whom he had formed. And out of the ground the Lord God made to spring up every tree that is pleasant to the sight and good for food."

It seems that before the flood, the dew and streams were enough to keep creation watered.

The Earth bears witness to the flood by its fossil record, showing billions and billions of items buried in sediment. On every continent, we find fossils of sea creatures in rock layers high above sea level. A good example is the  marine fossils found in the rock layers of the Grand Canyon and limestone beds high in the Himalaya Mountains (up to 30,000 feet above sea level). As water flooded the continents, it buried plants and animals in sediment layers rapidly. Many of the sediments were transported long distances from their original sources.

Keep in mind that things can happen fast. Jesus said that his second coming will be like the days of Noah.

> **"For the coming of the Son of Man will be just like the days of Noah. For as in those days before the flood they were eating and drinking, marrying and giving in marriage, until the day that Noah entered the ark, and they did not understand until the flood came and took them all away; so will the coming of the Son of Man be"** (Matt. 24:37–39).

Abraham (Abram) and his Descendants: Christianity and Islam

<u>*Abram*</u> was born in the city of Ur of the Chaldeans to a family that included older brothers Haran and Nahor (Genesis 11:26). Ur was the capital of the ancient kingdom of Sumer and was located about 200 miles southeast of Baghdad in lower Mesopotamia.

Abram's father was named <u>*Terah*</u>, and he had three sons—Abram, Nahor, and Haran. According to scripture, Terah was 130 years old when Abram was born. Abram lived in Ur until the age of seventy. After the death of the oldest son, Haran, Terah decided to take his remaining family to the city of Harran (also called Haran) in present-day Turkey.

Sarai was the wife of Abram, and both had the same father but different mothers (Genesis 20:12). God would later forbid marriage for those in that closeness of family. Still, it was not uncommon or disapproved of in Abram's day. Genetics then were purer than today, and intermarriage was not detrimental to the offspring of unions between relatives. Terah lived in Haran for five years and then died at the age of 205.

Abram and his father worshiped idols, but Abram's life changed when he was 75 years old when God told him, **"Go from your country, your people and your father's household to the land I will show you. I will make you into a great nation, and I will bless you; I will make your name great, and you will be a blessing"** (Joshua 24:2).

Abram was now directed to take his family, leave Haran, and go to Canaan—the Land of Promise. God also promised him, "*I will bless those who bless you, and whoever curses you I will curse; and all peoples on earth will be blessed through you*" (Genesis 12:1-2).

When Abram arrived in the promised land, God assured him that he and his descendants would be blessed. And the LORD said to Abram, **"Lift your eyes now and look from the place where you are—northward, southward, eastward,** *and westward; for all the land which you see I give to you and your descendants forever"* (Genesis 13).

Abram forsook moon idol worship, but worshiping heavenly objects became a continual problem with his descendants. Many times, in the Old Testament God rebuked the children of Abraham for their idolatry and renewed His call for them to worship Him alone.

The history of Abram is based on God's sovereign covenantal election of a people to be uniquely His. This kind of special relationship is scripturally termed a *covenant*. Abram entered into a covenant with God. God promised Abram that he would have an heir, *"One who will come from your own body"* (Genesis 15:4). God's promise was always fresh on Abram's mind, and it was a constant source of prayer and petition for both Abram and his wife Sarai. Yet, ten years after God's initial promise, no child had come. Sarai and Abram became impatient, and Sarai told Abram to take her Egyptian handmaid **Hagar** and produce a child by her.

This was a somewhat common practice at the time and was also practiced in Genesis 30 by Jacob's wives. The problem was that Abram and Sarai disobeyed God and His timeframe when they decided to fulfill His promise by having a child through Hagar. Abram slept with Hagar, and she became pregnant. In time, Sarai became jealous, dealt harshly with her, and Hagar fled into the desert. The angel of the Lord found Hagar in the desert and told her to return to Sarai. He said, *"You are now pregnant and will give birth to a son. You shall name him* **Ishmael** (means God listens, to hear), *for the Lord has heard of your misery. He will be a wild donkey of a man; his hand will be against everyone and everyone's hand against him, and he will live in hostility toward all his brothers"* (Genesis 16:11-12).

Hagar went back and bore the son Ishmael. Abram was eighty-six years old when Hagar bore this child. By tradition, the firstborn son was the one who would receive the inheritance and succeed the father as head of the household.

God appeared to Abram and once again promised to be the Father of Many Nations. God told Abram that Sarai, who was

90 years old, would have a son. Abram had difficulty believing this and asked God to fulfill His promises through Ishmael (verse 18). But God said the promise would be fulfilled through a son that Sarai would have, and his name would be **_Isaac_**. God would establish an everlasting covenant for Isaac and all his descendants.

> And God said, "*As for Ishmael, I have heard you: I will surely bless him; I will make him fruitful and greatly increase his numbers. He will be the father of twelve rulers, and I will make him into a great nation. <u>But my covenant I will establish with Isaac, whom Sarah will bear to you by this time next year</u>*" (vs. 19–21).

Fourteen years after the birth of Ishmael, God graced Abram with a second son, conceived with his wife Sarai. God instructed them to name this son Isaac, meaning one who laughs. At this time, God renamed **Abram** (exalted father) to **Abraham** (father of a great multitude of nations) and ***Sarai*** (*my princess*) to **Sarah** (*princess*).

After Isaac's birth, Sarah resented Hagar and Ishmael's presence and had them sent away (Genesis 21:8–13). God told Abraham, "*Do not let it be displeasing in your sight because of the lad or your bondwoman. Whatever Sarah has said to you, listen to her voice; for in Isaac your seed shall be called. Yet I will also make a nation of the son of the bondwoman, because he is your seed.*"

Abraham gathered some provisions and sent Hagar and Ishmael away. They set out initially for Egypt, in the direction of Beersheba, Hagar's homeland. It was a long and arduous journey through the Shur Desert, East of the Gulf of Suez, which stretched across the northern part of the Sinai Peninsula. The mother and son made it approximately 80 miles before they collapsed from the desert heat.

Hagar and Ishmael were overcome with grief, assuming that they would die in the desert. God heard the boy crying, and the angel of the Lord called to Hagar from heaven and said to her, "*What is the matter, Hagar? Do not be afraid; God has heard the boy crying as he lies there. Lift the boy up and take him by the hand, for I will make him into a great nation.*"

Then God opened her eyes, and she saw a well of water. She went and filled the skin with water and gave the boy a drink. Once again, God appeared to Hagar and promised that Ishmael would be a great nation. Hagar named the area where she encountered God "*Beer Lahai Roi*"— "*the Well of Him that Lives and Sees Me*" or "*the Well of the Vision of Life.*" The exact location is mentioned twice, as is where Isaac lived (Genesis 21).

As is typical of God, He takes a bad situation and works it for His glory. Hagar and Ishmael would be divinely cared for and protected. Scripture indicates that they continued their journey to Egypt and settled in the wilderness or desert of Paran. Ishmael became an archer, married an Egyptian woman, and fathered twelve sons. God used this scenario with Ishmael to establish yet another nation through His servant Abraham.

In Genesis 22, God tested Abraham's faith by commanding him to sacrifice his only son, Isaac. Isaac was the sole rightful heir promised to Abraham, through whom he would become the father of many nations. Abraham loaded provisions on his donkey and took Isaac along with two of his servants on a three-day journey up into the Moriah region. Abraham built an altar, cut enough wood for the burnt offering, and then tied Isaac on top of the wood. As he raised his knife to sacrifice his son to God, an angel of the Lord commanded him to stop. Through his actions, Abraham proved his fear and faith in God. A ram caught by his horns in a thicket became the burnt offering instead of Isaac. "*The LORD Will Provide*" is what Abraham called that place. Abraham's offspring worldwide would be blessed based on his faith and allegiance to God. Later, **Isaac had a son, Jacob—named Israel,** who is called the father of the Israelites.

When Sarah died, she was 127 years old, and Abraham took another wife (concubine) named Keturah. She bore him Zimran, Jokshan, Medan, Midian, Ishbak, and Shuah. Abraham had eight sons: Ishmael with **Hagar**, Isaac with **Sarah**, Zimran, Jokshan, Medan, Midian, Ishbak, and Shuah with **Keturah**.

After Sarah's death, Abraham sent his trusted servant **Eliezer,** who would have inherited Abraham's fortune if Ishmael and Isaac had not been born, to his relatives in Haran, Mesopotamia. He instructed Eliezer to bring back a bride for Isaac because he didn't want his son to marry any of the local Canaanite girls, because the Canaanites worshipped false gods. Abraham wanted Isaac to marry a righteous woman who would help him remain faithful to the living God and who would teach their children the truth.

God directed the quest, and with 10 loaded camels, Eliezer traveled some 450 miles. There, he found **Rebekah (Rebecca)** in the town of Nahor. Rebekah revealed she was a cousin and God's chosen wife for Isaac. <u>Rebekah returned with Eliezer and married Isaac</u> (vs. 60–67). Isaac was 60 years old when he became the father of twins—***Jacob and Esau*** (e-saw). While Isaac favored his elder son Esau, Rebekah's favorite was Jacob.

Through deception, Jacob, the younger son, received the inheritance and his father's blessing that should have gone to the older son, Esau. Abraham was 175 years old when he died, and he left everything he owned to Isaac, who was then about 75 years old. But while Abraham was still living, he gave many gifts to the sons of his concubines.

The descendants of Ishmael and those of Isaac had historically been enemies. Still, it is interesting that Isaac and Ishmael reunited, and together they buried Abraham in the *Cave of Machpelah* near Mamre (Genesis 25:9). Although many Jewish people want to enter the cave and pray, few are allowed. According to tradition, Abraham, Isaac, Jacob, along with their wives Sarah, Rebekah, and Leah, were buried in the cave, also known as the Cave of the Patriarchs, or Tomb of the Patriarchs.

Ishmael lived 137 years and had 12 sons (Genesis 25:12-18). ***The 12 Tribes of Abram, Hagar, and Ishmael*** are Nebajoth, Kedar, Adbeel, Mibsam, Mishma, Dumah, Massa, Hadar, Tema, Jetur, Naphish, and Kedemah.

These twelve tribes or nations of Ishmael would go on to populate what we know today as the territories of the Middle East, believed to be the Arabs. Additionally, the Bible states that the descendants of Ishmael would be princes, signifying royalty. And as God had earlier revealed, "they lived in hostility toward all the tribes related to them." The history of the Arab people attests to the accuracy of this prophecy about the descendants of Hagar and Ishmael.

Isaac followed God's commands, and his story illustrates God's faithfulness to His promises. God selected Isaac to carry on the covenant line that would lead to Jacob and ultimately the Messiah, Jesus.

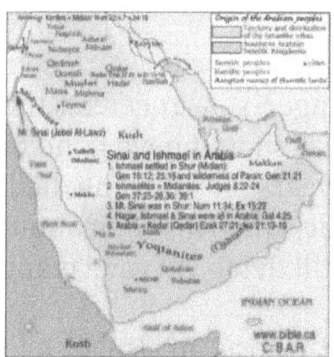
For many generations, the Jewish nation has referred to their God as the God of Abraham, Isaac, and Jacob.

The 12 Tribes of Abraham, Sarah, Isaac, Jacob (Israel) are Judah, Ephraim, Dan, Ephraim, Gad, Issachar, Manasseh, Naphtali, Reuben, Simeon, Zebulun, and Benjamin.

Abraham was the first of the Hebrew patriarchs and is revered by the three great monotheistic religions: Judaism, Christianity, and Islam.

Why are there three religions?

In Judaism, the promised offspring of the Jewish people is thought to descend from Abraham's son, Isaac, born of his wife Sarah.

In Christianity, the genealogy is traced back to Adam and Abraham and then to Jesus and his sacrifice on the cross.

The Islamic religion *centers* on Ishmael, Abram's firstborn son, born of Hagar, who is viewed as fulfilling God's promise, and the Prophet Muhammad is his purported descendant.

A Look at the Book of Job

Job is the central figure of the Book of Job. He is presented as a good and prosperous family man suddenly beset with horrendous disasters that take away all he holds dear. The catastrophes are intended to test Job's faith in God. Struggling to understand this situation, Job reflects on his despair and tries to remain devout and faithful to God.

The story begins with Job being described as a blessed man who lives righteously in the Land of Uz. The exact location of the land of Uz is uncertain, but scripture states that Job lived near the desert; yet the territory was fertile for farming and raising livestock (Job 1:3–19).

Job's homeland was also vulnerable to Chaldean raiding parties. So, if these pieces are put together, the land of Uz appears to have been located to the east of the land of Israel and east of Edom in northern Saudi Arabia.

There are several theories about where the tribe of Job was from, including *Bedad, Edom, Midianites*, and the descendants of *Bedad*. Job's father was **Zerah**, from Esau's lineage, and his mother was **Bosorrha**. They were natives of Bozrah, and Job was the fifth generation from Abraham.

At the start of this story, Job has seven sons, three daughters, and his estate includes 7,000 sheep, 3,000 camels, 500 yoke of oxen, 500 female donkeys, and a very large number of servants. Job was the greatest man among all the people of the East. When family birthday feasts were held, it was Jobs' custom to sacrifice a *"purifying"* burnt offering for each of the children. This was done just in case the children had sinned and cursed God in their hearts.

"Now there was a day when the sons of God came to present themselves before the LORD, and Satan came also among them" (Job 1:6).

Some say that the *"sons of God"* are angelic beings; if so, it is unclear if they are fallen and/or unfallen angels. Notice it says that they *"present themselves before the LORD."* Since God made all beings, they are accountable to God for their good and evil actions. God could ensure they act within the parameters He set (Gen 6:1–4).

And keep in mind that Satan (the adversary and accuser) may be powerful, but what he can and can't do is also controlled by God. Perhaps Satan and the others report to God in unspecified intervals.

God asked Satan where he had come from, and Satan replied, **"From roaming throughout the earth, going back and forth on it."** Satan is called the *"prince of the power of the air"* (Ephesians 2:2) and the *"ruler of this world"* (John 12:31).

God then asked Satan, **"Have you considered my servant Job? There is no one on earth like him; he is blameless and upright, a man who fears God and shuns evil."**

Satan responded that God had put a protective hedge around Job and his family and that if God were to take that protection and his possessions away, Job would curse God.

This is where it gets very interesting. God says to Satan, **"Very well, then, everything Job has is in your power, but on the man himself do not lay a finger."** In other words, Satan could do what he wished with Job's property, but he could not harm or kill him. Satan then went out from the presence of the Lord.

What Job experienced next was somewhat like what happened in Egypt when the plagues occurred. A messenger came to Job and told him that the Sabeans had attacked and made off with the oxen they were using while plowing and the donkeys grazing nearby. They also killed all the servants, and the messenger was the only one who escaped. While Job was being told this, another messenger said that God's fire fell from the heavens and burned up all the sheep and servants, and he was the only one who escaped.

As this message was being relayed, another messenger came and told him that three Chaldean raiding parties stole all of Job's camels and killed all the servants. He was the only one who had escaped to tell Job. And even as this messenger was speaking, yet another messenger came and said that all of Jobs sons and daughters who were feasting and drinking wine at the oldest brother's house, were killed when a mighty wind swept in from the desert, struck the four corners of the house, and it collapsed on them. He was the only one to escape to tell Job.

When Job heard this news, he tore his robe, shaved his head, and fell to the ground in worship. He said, **"Naked I came from my mother's womb, and naked I will depart. The Lord gave and the Lord has taken away; may the name of the Lord be praised."** Job did not sin by charging God with any wrongdoing.

A first reaction by most people is, Why is God using Job in a test with Satan? It would seem that God is being very unfair to Job! You might even say that God provoked the testing.

Later, there was another day when the sons of God came to present themselves before the Lord, and Satan also came among them. And the Lord reminded Satan that even though he had sent much misery upon Job, it had not caused Job to lose faith in the Lord.

"Satan answered the Lord, and said, Skin for skin, yea, all that a man hath will he give for his life. But put forth thine hand now, and touch his bone and his flesh, and he will curse thee to thy face. And the Lord said unto Satan, Behold, he is in thine hand; but save his life."

Satan then caused Job to have boils all over his body. Job's wife did not encourage him and said, *"Dost thou still retain thine integrity? curse God, and die."* But Job rebuked her and said that she was speaking foolishly. He stated that if they receive good at the hand of God, should they also not receive bad? In all this, Job did not sin with his lips.

Job had three friends, **Eliphaz the Temanite** *(el-i-paz), Bildad the Shuhite (bil-dad), and Zophar the Naamathite (zo-par),* who heard of the misery that had come upon Job and came to comfort him. They sat with Job for seven days and seven nights, and no one spoke a word to him. After those seven days had passed, Job spoke and cursed the day he was born. If he had died at birth, he would now be at rest in the grave. He wondered why the miserable, who long for death, are nevertheless granted life. He had no peace.

His friend Eliphaz emphasized that no innocent person has ever suffered as much as Job, and that God has brought this punishment to chasten a sinful Job and restore him to righteousness.

As Job and his friends debate God's fairness, it becomes clear that they all believed in the false doctrine of *"retribution theology,"* which is the idea that you get what you deserve.

God sees that the good people get good things in life, and the bad people get bad things. God punishes people in this world in direct response to their actions. Job's friends assumed that Job's troubles resulted from his wickedness and that God always rewards the righteous and punishes the wicked. They repeatedly recommended that Job repent of his sins and seek God's favor.

Job tried to defend the complaints and criticized his friends for being unkind, treacherous, deceitful, and not helping him understand his faults. Job then challenged them to show him where he had sinned. Job complained of his hardships and prayed to be delivered from the sting of his afflictions. He pleaded with God and complained of the severity of his afflictions. Jobs' friends claimed his words displayed arrogance and a lack of repentance. They stressed that Job's sufferings were well deserved but far less severe than he probably deserved.

They repeatedly stressed that Job should confess and repent of his sins, and then God would bless, honor, and restore him to his admired life again.

At this point, Job sarcastically called his friends "*the people of wisdom*" and reminded them that wisdom belongs to God. Again, he stated that his suffering resulted from what God had done, not because of his failings. Job said that his friends' explanations were unrealistic and did not account for the mysteries of God's ways.

Job then accused his friends of being liars and worthless physicians and asked them to be silent and listen to his reasoning. He expressed his confidence in God and his desire to know his sins. His friends continued to accuse him of being punished by God for his wrongdoing. They also charged Job with not fearing God and said that he would leave no good memories when he died. Job cried for a heavenly witness to vouch for him so that he could prove his innocence.

Job was now just about at his wits' end and complained of the torment his friends had brought him and God's treatment of him. He felt his friends had abandoned him, reaffirming his desire to plead his case before God. He thought that if this could happen, God would listen to his arguments and acquit him. Job had by now lost interest in answering all the unjust accusations by his friends. Satan continued to test Job's faithfulness.

Job highlighted God's greatness and purity, but his friends said that Job should not try to present his case before God because, with God's greatness and power, man can't be justified or clean before Him. Job said that his friends didn't understand God's ways and declared that even though God was the master of the universe, he still deserved some explanation.

Job remembered his relationship with God, his family, and his former honorable place in the community. He had helped the poor and wretched and was "clothed" with righteousness and justice. Because of these things, Job felt confident that he would live long and die peacefully. The people thought well of him, and now he grieved for the honorable life he once enjoyed. His world had turned upside down, and he went from enjoying *"the respect of the most respectable"* to undergoing *"the contempt of the most contemptible."*

At this point, **Elihu** (e–li–hu), son of Barakel the Buzite of the family of Ram (the youngest of Job's friends), visited Job. Elihu becomes very angry with Job for justifying himself rather than God, and he is also furious with the three friends because they have done nothing but condemn Job. Elihu had waited before speaking to Job because Job's friends were older and thought they were wiser than Elihu. He then stated that he could add wisdom to the conversation, which Job's friends had failed to do.

Elihu again reprimanded Job for justifying himself and advised him to patiently submit to the suffering he was under. He then offered advice that would benefit Job and bring glory to God. He urged Job to consider God's wondrous works and acknowledge His incomprehensible power, majesty, justice, and fearfulness.

Suddenly, the scene changes, and from within a whirlwind (storm), God responds to Job's complaints and challenges Job to answer His questions. ***"Gird up now thy loins like a man; for I will demand of thee, and answer thou me"*** (Job 38:3).

This implies that Job needs to be ready for a serious and challenging conversation with God, who will demand of him and question him. God starts by asking Job if he was present at the creation of the earth and if he had set boundaries for the sea, again emphasizing His power and control over nature.

God asked Job if he had ever commanded the day and night cycles or shown his knowledge of the unexplored and unknown. God asked Job if he knew how to control light and darkness, again highlighting His omnipresence (being present anywhere and everywhere) and Job's limited understanding. God challenged Job's knowledge of natural elements like the weather, such as snow, rain, lightning, and constellations, further illustrating His sovereign rule over all creation.

God then questioned Job about his knowledge of feeding the wild animals, his understanding of the universe, and his questioning of divine justice. God emphasized His omnipotence (having unlimited power) and omniscience (knowing everything). God spoke to Job about His power and wisdom over everything and challenged Job to show his righteousness, power, and wisdom and answer any of these questions.

God then further illustrated His power by describing *Behemoth (be-he-moth)*, a large and mighty creature, and a dragon-like creature called Leviathan (la-vi-a-than) that is so powerful that no human can tame or defeat it—yet each of them is under God's control.

In his misery, Job had charged God with injustice and wanted a trial, yet in this trial, we see Job has no legal standing to convict God. Job cannot explain how God controls the universe, and he cannot present any evidence of injustice. Also, God had established His absolute right to do what He wants. At this point, Job is humbled and pledges his loyalty to God. He thinks of himself as a sinner at heart and in life, especially for speaking against God. He is shameful.

The Lord asked Job, **"Will the one who contends with the Almighty correct him? Let him who accuses God answer him!"** (Job 40:2-5). Then Job answered the Lord, **"I am** *unworthy—how can I reply to you? I put my hand over my mouth. I spoke once, but I have no answer— twice, but I will say no more."*

After the Lord had spoken to Job, He said to Eliphaz the Temanite, *"My anger burns against you and against your two friends, for you have not spoken of me what is right, as my servant Job has. Therefore, take seven bulls and seven rams and go to my servant Job and offer up a burnt offering for yourselves* (Job 42:7-8).

As God spoke to Job, you may have felt that God was "against" Job rather than "for" him. But as we look back at Job and his friend Elihu's discussions, we see that Elihu may have served a dual role, serving under the Holy Spirit's inspiration as Job's advocate before God and God's advocate before Job (Job 32-37).

According to Elihu, he was inspired to speak the wisdom Job's friends lacked. He said, *"One who is perfect in knowledge is with you."* Perhaps Elihu was confident about the knowledge God had revealed for this situation.

Elihu denounced Job's friends for their inability to help and said that God uses suffering as a means of teaching, not just as a means of punishment. His main point was not that Job must be guilty, but that God's majesty is greater than human understanding. This is close to God's argument, and when God calls Job's friends to repent of their words, He omits Elihu.

Job's brothers, sisters, and acquaintances came to his home to comfort him over all his troubles. Every man gave Job a piece of silver (money), and everyone gave an earring of gold (some say a gold ring). It is thought that these gifts were simply an expression of love and support for Job because of the difficult times he experienced.

Scripture states that the Lord didn't just restore Job to his earlier condition but blessed him with twice as much as he had before. God blessed Job with fourteen thousand sheep, six thousand camels, a thousand yoke of oxen, a thousand female donkeys, and a great household.

Job had ten children, and after his tragic loss of everything, he lived long enough to father ten more children and amass even greater wealth. Jobs' final three daughters were named *Jemimah* (dove), *Keziah* (cassia tree; sweet-scented spice cinnamon), and *Keren-Happuch* (horn of antimony—eye makeup). His daughters were said to be the most beautiful women in the land.

Job lived an additional 140 years after "all these things," seeing his children and grandchildren for four generations (Job 42:16-17). It is thought that Job would have been about 70 years old when his trials befell him, which would make him between 210 and 240 years old when he died.

The Bible does not list the death of Job's wife as a part of any of the curses brought upon Job by Satan. While the Bible records the death of Job's children, Job's wife is alive during his suffering because she speaks harsh words to him. Because the Book of Job never records her death or indicates that Job  remarried, the assumption is that the same woman who bore Job his first ten children, who were killed, also bore him ten more children after he was restored.

Many scholars believe the Book of Job is the oldest in the Bible, but no one knows for sure because the ancient world did not have books and authors as we do today. These were days when speaking and hearing dominated the culture. Since some of the oldest events in the Bible take place in Genesis, many scholars believe this to be the oldest book. Others will point out that the book of Job appears to record events that took place before Moses. This debate continues.

It is possible that Job lived sometime between the flood and Moses's time. One clue that places Job in the time before Moses is the fact that Job gave his daughters "an inheritance among their brothers" (Job 42:15). Under the Mosaic Law, a father passed his inheritance to sons only unless he had no sons (Numbers 27:1-11). A righteous man like Job would have followed that law in obedience to God.

Few of us possess the patience of Job. Job exhibited great endurance in his affliction: "You have heard of Job's perseverance and have seen what the Lord finally brought about" (James 5:11).

We know that Job suffered for much longer than a week because when Job's three friends arrived, they sat on the ground with him for seven days and seven nights — in total silence. The friends first had to learn of Job's suffering before traveling to meet him, and we don't know the timeframe when God questioned Job.

Interestingly, in Judaism, Job is cited as someone "who held fast to all the ways of justice." In Mormonism, he is mentioned in the Doctrine and Covenants, one of the four sacred texts of the Church of Jesus Christ of Latter-day Saints. In the Islamic Quran, he is called the Prophet Ayūb, a righteous servant of Allah, and Christianity accepts the Book of Job as canon in its Old Testament.

Many think that one of the book of Job's main points is to challenge the false teaching of "retribution theology," the idea that God blesses the righteous and punishes the wicked in this life.

I once read that bad things happen to good people — because good people don't exist. Why would someone say something that harsh? Although God created us in His image, and we mean a great deal to Him, we have fallen and are under the curse, so perhaps we really can't be classified as "good" or morally perfect people.

We all live by God's mercy, and many of the bad things or disasters we experience serve God's sovereign purpose; they may be object lessons to warn us about the far greater eternal disasters of Hell. In many cases, those who have greatly suffered have also become more receptive to the gospel, drawing them closer to God. Perhaps when we experience these difficult times, we should ask God, "What are you trying to tell me?" When we are tempted to ask God, "Why did you do this to me?" it may be more fruitful to look at the cross and ask, "Why did you do this for me?"

God found fault in Job failing to recognize that he has no right to pass judgment on the wisdom and goodness of an infinite creator. ***Do we as "the clay" think we can criticize the work of "the potter?"***

God demonstrated to Job and Satan that He controls all things. God exists outside of time and sees the beginning and the end of everything in full view. God talks about Job's faith and his being blameless, but makes no mention of His wager with Satan. This is the issue that most of us would probably be questioning. The sovereign God knew what Job needed to know, and likewise, He knows what you and I need to know.

I have read this story many times and was always troubled that God didn't respond to why there was a wager with Satan, or Job's questions about his miseries, or the family deaths. ***But after reading the response Job gave to God, I better understand that if Job was satisfied with God's answer… then we should be too.***

If God had explained his wager with Satan, it would have probably raised more questions than answers. Rather than presenting "**WHY**" the sovereign God reveals "**WHO**" by stating his greatness as the creator of everything. Additional answers are unnecessary except to show that all-powerful God will always help us through our pain and suffering.

As we close this study, there are a few key thoughts to remember:

1. When we have a crisis, we need to pour out our hearts to God—He can handle our grief and anger,

2. We should never turn from God and be bitter,

3. We should never insist on taking command. Let God's plan work the issue,

4. We should always trust that God is working behind the scenes and will reveal His plan to us one day.

So, as we end Job's story, even though Job was greatly rewarded, he never found out why he suffered the afflictions. We learned that bad things do happen to good people and that even though our friends may sometimes fail us, God never does. The story teaches us about the nature of suffering, the character of God, and the importance of faith.

The Book of Job also reminds us that there is a "cosmic conflict" going on behind the scenes that we know nothing about. We often wonder why God allows something to happen, and then we question or doubt God's goodness without seeing the whole picture.

This story teaches us to trust God under ALL circumstances. Suffering may sometimes be allowed to purify, test, teach, or strengthen the soul. We must trust God, and He reminds us:

"For my thoughts are not your thoughts, neither are your ways my ways. For as the heavens are higher than the earth, so are my ways higher than your ways and my thoughts than your thoughts" (Isaiah 55:8-9).

Things You May Not Know About Moses

Believe it or not, **Moses** was famous long before Cecil B. DeMille made the movie, *The Ten Commandments*, starring Charlton Heston. Moses is one of the most prominent figures in the Old Testament and was chosen by God to bring  redemption to His people. The story of Moses is a classic tale of having faith in God and begins in the Book of Exodus.

Much debate has occurred about the meaning of "Moses." According to the Torah, the name Moses comes from the Hebrew verb "Moshe," meaning "to pull out/draw out" of water, and the infant Moses was given this name by Pharaoh's daughter (Exodus 2:10). The name Moses, which has a similar pronunciation, is linked to the Egyptian word "Mes," meaning "son." Still, it could also be associated with "deliverance" or "savior."

Moses' father was a Levite named **Amram**, a son of Kohath, one of the three Levitical clans. Amram married his father's sister **Jochebed**, a Levite, who bore him **Aaron** and **Moses**.

At this time, lawful marriages between close relatives were not uncommon; however, marriages between close relatives were later forbidden in the Mosaic Law. Moses was born several years after their marriage because Jochebed already had a daughter (**Miriam**) who was old enough at the time of Moses' infancy to act as a lookout in Exodus 2:4. Miriam the prophetess, is mentioned by name in Exodus 15:20. Aaron was thought to be about three years old when Moses was born.

Egyptian history about the Pharaohs is challenging. Some say that *Pharaoh Seti I* drove Israel into deeper slavery and *Rameses II* was the Pharaoh defeated in the days of Moses. But other scholars seem to think that the Pharoah Moses dealt with was the son of Rameses II: *Merneptah.* Regardless, the acting Pharaoh turned the Hebrew people into slaves and used them to work on his massive building projects. Over time, the Egyptians began to fear the increasing number of Jews living in their land, and Pharaoh ordered the death of all newly born male Hebrew children.

"Then Pharaoh gave this order to all his people: "Every Hebrew boy that is born you must throw into the Nile but let every girl live" (Exodus 1:22).

To save her child, Jochebed placed Moses in a papyrus basket coated with tar and pitch and put the basket among the reeds along the bank of the Nile River. When Pharaoh's daughter went to the Nile to bathe, she saw the basket among the reeds and sent her female slave to get it. She opened the basket, saw the baby, and felt sorry for him.

"This is one of the Hebrew babies," she said. Miriam watched and asked Pharaoh's daughter, *"Shall I go and get one of the Hebrew women to nurse the baby for you?"* In this act in Exodus 2:7-9, the mother Jochebed became Moses' nurse and was paid by the king for her service. You might say that Moses was the first abandoned child mentioned in the Bible.

Pharaoh's daughter adopted Moses and raised him in the palace. Moses probably lived in the palace for about 35 years. As part of the royal family, Moses was brought up in the splendor of the Egyptian court. As Moses grew older, he had much sympathy for the plight of his people.

One day, he became furious while witnessing an Egyptian master brutally beating a Hebrew slave, and he impulsively killed the Egyptian and hid the body in the sand. Exodus 2:15 states that Moses, fearing that the Pharaoh would kill him, fled to the land of Midian, where he worked as a shepherd. Here he met the daughters of Jethro, the priest of Midian. The daughters had come to draw water and fill the troughs to water their father's flock. Some shepherds came along and drove them away, but Moses defended the daughters and watered their flock. Moses eventually married one of the daughters named **_Zipporah_**. Together, they had a son named **_Gershom_** (*a stranger there*) because Moses said, "I have become a foreigner in a foreign land," and a son named **_Eliezer_** (*God is my help*). Moses said, "My father's God was my helper; he saved me from the sword of Pharaoh." Moses lived in Midian for about forty-plus years.

Moses was tending to the flock of Jethro, his father-in-law, near Mount Horeb, another name for Mount Sinai. This is the same mountain where the Hebrew people entered into a covenant with God after escaping from bondage in Egypt, and it is also the place where Moses received the Ten Commandments (Deuteronomy 5:2).

Moses caught sight of a bush that was on fire but not burning up. God spoke to him from the flames as he was investigating the phenomenon. Calling him by name, the Lord told Moses, **"take off your sandals, for the place where you are standing is holy ground."** The Lord said, **"I am the God of your father, the God of Abraham, the God of Isaac and the God of Jacob."** This name emphasized God's covenant with Israel and the Israelites' special place as God's chosen people.

God told Moses that He had seen the misery of His people in Egypt, and that He was sending Moses to the Pharaoh, *"to bring my people the Israelites out of Egypt."* Interestingly, Moses made several excuses for why he shouldn't go, such as, *"Who am I that I should go to Pharaoh and bring the Israelites out of Egypt?"* God said, *"I will go with you."*

Moses said, *"Suppose I go to the Israelites and say to them, 'The God of your fathers has sent me to you,' and they ask me, 'What is his name?' Then what shall I tell them?* God said to tell them, **"I AM"** *has sent me to you. Tell them the God of your fathers—the God of Abraham, the God of Isaac and the God of Jacob has sent me to you."*

Moses then said, *"What if they do not believe me or listen to me and say, The Lord did not appear to you?"* The Lord asked Moses what was in his hand, and it was a staff. The Lord said, *"throw the staff on the ground, and when he did it became a snake."* When Moses took the snake by the tail, it turned back into a staff in his hand.

The Lord then told Moses to put his hand in his cloak, and when he did and took it out, the skin was leprous — it had become as white as snow. When Moses put his hand back into his cloak and took it out, it was restored, like the rest of his flesh.

The Lord then told Moses, if the Egyptians still do not believe you, *"Take some water from the Nile and pour it on the dry ground. The water you take from the river will become blood on the ground."*

Moses told the Lord, *"Pardon your servant, Lord. I have never been eloquent, neither in the past nor since you have spoken to your servant. I am slow of speech and tongue."* The Lord said He would help him speak and teach him what to say. Moses said, *"Pardon your servant, Lord. Please send someone else."*

The Lord's anger burned against Moses, and he said, *"What about your brother, Aaron the Levite? I know he can speak well. He is already on his way to meet you, and he will be glad to see you. You shall speak to him and put words in his mouth; I will help both of you speak and will teach you what to do. He will speak to the people for you, and it will be as if he were your mouth and as if you were God to him. But take this staff in your hand so you can perform the signs with it."*

The Lord told Moses, *"Go back to Egypt, for all those who wanted to kill you are dead."* So, Moses took his wife Zipporah and their two sons and began to travel to Egypt.

It's interesting that at a lodging place on the way, the Lord was about to kill Moses because he had not circumcised his son Gershom. Circumcision was the sign of the covenant between God and the descendants of Abraham (Genesis 17:9–14). Any uncircumcised male must be *"cut off from his people."* This could mean banishment or even death. Before Moses could assume leadership, he had to get his house in order. Scripture says that Moses' wife, Zipporah, angrily took a flint knife, circumcised the child, and then touched Moses' feet with the foreskin—an act that "healed" Moses because it was tangible evidence that the sinful situation had been corrected. Zipporah said to Moses, "You are a bridegroom of blood to me," referring to the circumcision incident.

It is thought that this was probably when Zipporah and her two sons were sent back to Jethro in Midian. They stayed in Jethro's care until God miraculously delivered the Hebrew people out of slavery in Egypt. Jethro later returned Zipporah, Gershom, and Eliezer to Moses.

When Moses and Aaron arrived in Egypt, they made their request to Pharaoh. But the Lord had made the Pharaoh's heart hard, and each time they made the request to release the people, Pharaoh refused. And each time he refused, God issued a plague on the Egyptian people. The ten plagues of Egypt, as described in occurred in the following order (Exodus 7–8):

The Plague of Blood: "With the staff that is in my hand, I will strike the water of the Nile, and all waters of Egypt will be changed into blood. Blood will be everywhere in Egypt, even in vessels of wood and stone."

The Plague of Frogs: It is said that this frog plague consisted of frogs escaping the polluted Nile and invading all of Egypt, including people's homes. A Rabbinic source stated that if the Egyptians tried to kill a frog by striking it, the frog split into swarms each time it was struck.

The Plague of Gnats: God instructed Moses and Aaron to strike the dust of the ground with a staff, and the dust turned into gnats that infested people and animals. The plague of gnats could also cause diseases such as spotted fever, which is transmitted by the insect's fluids and excrement.

The Plague of Flies: Swarms of flies ruined the land throughout Egypt.

The Plague upon Livestock: This was on all the horses, donkeys, camels, cattle, sheep, and goats. But the LORD made a distinction between the livestock of Israel and that of Egypt, so that no animal belonging to the Israelites died.

The Plague of Boils: God commanded Moses and Aaron to take two handfuls of soot from the kiln and had Moses throw it skyward, thus spreading the bubonic plague all over Egypt. This plague is caused by a bacterium called Yersinia pestis and is characterized by chills, fever, vomiting, diarrhea, and the formation of black boils in the armpits, neck, and groin.

The Plague of Hail: The Lord rained hail upon the land of Egypt, and it struck down everything that was in the field in all the land of Egypt, both man and beast.

The Plague of Locusts: God brought locusts into the land, and they covered the face of the ground. They devoured all that was left after the hail.

The Plague of Darkness: This was a thick darkness that lasted for three days and prevented any movement or activity.

The Plague of the Firstborn: This was the tenth and final plague that God sent to Egypt to free the Israelites from slavery. God told Moses that he would strike every firstborn son in Egypt, from Pharaoh to the slave, and the firstborn of the cattle.

Before this final plague, God commanded Moses that the Jewish people were to select a lamb and slaughter it. They were to eat the lamb with unleavened bread and bitter herbs, such as the **Passover** meal or "*Pesach*," which means "pass over." The Jewish people were to take a bunch of hyssops, then dip them into the lamb's blood, and then put some of the blood on the top and both sides of the doorframe. When the angel of the Lord went through the land to strike down the Egyptians, he would pass over those homes that had the blood on the doorframe.

This *"destroying angel"* is sometimes called the *"angel of death."* However, no biblical evidence exists that any one angel was given the title "destroying angel" or "angel of death."

All the Egyptian firstborn children behind the unmarked doorways died at midnight, causing grief and great wailing in Egypt (Exodus 12:21-29). At this point, the Pharaoh sent for Moses and Aaron and told them to take their people out of his country and leave them alone. The next morning, the people took unleavened bread dough with their kneading bowls on their shoulders as they left Egypt. The Lord also made the Egyptians disposed toward the people, and they gave them articles of silver, gold, and clothing.

Although questioned by some scholars, Exodus 12:37 states that the Israelites were about six hundred thousand men on foot, not including women and children. Other people joined them, and there were also large droves of livestock, both flocks and herds.

It wasn't long before Pharaoh and his officials changed their minds about letting the people go because they realized they had lost most of their slave labor.  Pharaoh took 600 of his best men, with horses and chariots, and pursued the Israelites. They overtook the people as they camped by the Red Sea near *Pi Hahiroth*, opposite *Baal Zephon*. The Israelites saw the Egyptians approaching and were terrified.

> They asked Moses, *"Was it because there were no graves in Egypt that you brought us to the desert to die? It would have been better for us to serve the Egyptians than to die in the desert!"*

Moses told the people not to be afraid, and they would see the deliverance the Lord would bring to them that day. Then the angel of God, who had been traveling with the people, caused a pillar of cloud between the army of Egypt and the Israelites. Throughout the night, the cloud brought darkness to one side and light to the other side, so neither went near the other all night long.

Moses stretched out his hand over the Red Sea, and the Lord drove the water back with a strong east wind. The sea was divided, and the Israelites passed through on dry ground, with a wall of water on each side. When Pharaoh's army later followed them onto the dry land, the Lord told Moses to stretch out his hand over the sea so that the waters might flow back over the Egyptians, their chariots, and horsemen. The water flowed back, covering the entire army of Pharaoh, and nothing survived.

The Israelites saw the Lord's mighty hand displayed against the Egyptians and feared Him, putting their trust in Him and Moses, his servant. Moses was 80 years old when he led the children of Israel out of Egypt.

The Staff: God demonstrated His power by performing miracles using Moses' rod or staff, but He also used the staff of Moses' brother  Aaron for miracles. In Pharaoh's court, the Egyptian magi had turned their staffs into snakes, and the snake that had been Aaron's staff swallowed theirs up (Exodus 7:8–10). It was Aaron's staff that God used to turn the water of Egypt into blood and summon the plagues of the frogs and the gnats.

In Numbers 16–17, Aaron's staff was part of another famous story involving the Levites. A few group members, Korah, Dathan, and Abiram, became disgruntled over the extra authority granted to Moses and Aaron, inciting a rebellion with 250 other followers. They contended for the priesthood and challenged Moses' authority. The Lord punished the rebels by causing the earth to swallow them and their families, and by sending fire and a plague that killed 14,700 others. Moses and Aaron interceded for the people, stopping the plague.

To end the unrest, God once again used Aaron's staff for a miracle. God commanded Moses to have the leader of each tribe of Israel bring his staff to the tent of meeting, with Aaron's staff representing the tribe of Levi. Each of the twelve leaders had their name inscribed on his staff.

The Lord told Moses that buds would sprout on the staff belonging to the man He chose. In the morning, Aaron's staff, representing the tribe of Levi, had sprouted, blossomed, and produced ripe almonds. Moses was then instructed to place Aaron's staff permanently into the **Ark of the Covenant** to warn rebels (Hebrews 9:4). Aaron's staff remained in the Ark of the Covenant as a testimony of God's choice of Aaron and Moses to lead His people. Aaron's staff was also a reminder that God does not put up with rebellion against Himself or His chosen representatives here on earth (1 Corinthians 10:10).

The people were supposed to take possession of the land God had promised their forefathers; a land *"flowing with milk and honey"* (Exodus 3:8). Upon their arrival at *Kadesh Barnea*, which bordered the Promised Land of Canaan, Moses sent out twelve spies to survey the land and its people. After forty days of exploration, the spies returned and stated that the people were of great size and could not be removed from the land, even though God told them they could. Only **_Joshua_** and **_Caleb_** believed what the Lord had said. The other people lost heart and rebelled. Their lack of belief in God's word and promises brought forth the wrath of God. ***He cursed them with forty years of wilderness wandering (one year for each of the forty days they explored the land)*** until the unbelieving generation had died, never stepping foot in the Promised Land.

The ten men who had given the bad report were struck down and died of a plague before the Lord. Only Joshua, son of Nun, and Caleb, son of Jephunneh, survived. These were the two faithful spies who believed God's promise to give the land over to them (Numbers 14:34–37).

An incident at Meribah/Massah also taught Moses that certain sins may continue to haunt you throughout your life. Nearing the end of their forty years of wandering, the Israelites came to the Desert of Zin. There was no water, and the people became very angry. God told Moses and Aaron to gather the assembly, speak to the rock, and water would come forth. Moses took the staff and gathered the men, but in anger, Moses struck the rock twice with his staff (Numbers 20:10-11). Water came from the rock, but Moses had disobeyed a direct command from God to speak to the rock instead of striking it with his staff. Earlier, when God had brought water from a rock, He had instructed Moses to strike it with his staff, but God's instructions were different here (Exodus 17).

Also, Moses (and Aaron) seemed to be taking credit for the miracle themselves, instead of attributing it to God. Because of this, both Moses and Aaron were guilty of unbelief and disobedience and were prohibited from entering the Promised Land. Moses called the place Meribah, which means "quarrelling," and Massah, which means "testing."

The Feast of the Passover and the Feast of the Unleavened Bread celebrate the Israelites' exodus from Egypt and their freedom from slavery to the Egyptians.

Commemorations today involve a special meal called the "**Seder**," featuring unleavened bread and other food items symbolic of various aspects of the exodus. Passover is one of the most widely celebrated Jewish holidays, along with **Shavuot** (the Feast of Weeks or Pentecost) and **Sukkot** (the Feast of Tabernacles). Passover is one of the three "pilgrimage" festivals in Scripture, during which the Jews were commanded to travel to Jerusalem and observe the feasts together. Passover takes place in the spring, during the Hebrew month of Nisan.

*Most people don't know that Moses helped Joshua fight the Amalekites. Aaron and a man named Hur held up Moses' hands in a battle with the Amalekites, so that the Israelite forces miraculously prevailed (Exodus 17:10-13).

> *"So Joshua fought the Amalekites as Moses had ordered, and Moses, Aaron and Hur went to the top of the hill. As long as Moses held up his hands, the Israelites were winning, but whenever he lowered his hands, the Amalekites were winning. When Moses' hands grew tired, they took a stone and put it under him, and he sat on it. Aaron and Hur held his hands up—one on one side, one on the other—so that his hands remained steady till sunset. So, Joshua overcame the Amalekite army with the sword."*

Moses went up on Mount Sinai <u>eight times</u> to meet God.
On the <u>first ascent</u> after the exodus from Egypt, God tells Moses that He is offering a covenant to the people of Israel. If they keep the covenant, God will make them His *"treasured possession"* and *"a kingdom of priests and a holy nation."* Moses reports this message to the people, who respond, *"We will do everything the Lord has said"* (Exodus 9:2-11).

On the <u>second ascent,</u> God tells Moses that He will speak audibly to Moses in a thick cloud so that all the people will trust Moses as God's chosen leader.

The <u>third ascent</u> describes Moses consecrating the people in preparation for the Lord's appearance on the mountain. On the third day, *"there was thunder and lightning, with a thick cloud over the mountain, and a very loud trumpet blast"* (Exodus 19:16). Mount Sinai was covered with smoke because the Lord descended on it in fire, and the whole mountain trembled violently.

During the <u>fourth ascent,</u> God told Moses to warn the people not to draw near the mountain while His presence was on Sinai. God then delivered the Ten Commandments audibly (Exodus 20:1-17). In fear, the people of Israel pleaded with Moses not to let God speak directly to them. Instead, they asked Moses to be their intercessor.

In the <u>fifth ascent</u>, God gives Moses various laws and promises to give the land of Canaan to the children of Israel (Exodus 23:20-33).

In the sixth ascent, God summons Moses, Aaron, his sons Nadab and Abihu, and seventy of the elders of Israel (Exodus 24:8).

The next morning, Moses *"built an altar at the foot of the mountain and set up twelve stone pillars representing the twelve tribes of Israel."* He offered burnt offerings and sacrificed young bulls as fellowship offerings to the Lord and read the *Book of the Covenant* (thought to be rules or text appearing in the Torah) to the people, who responded, *"We will do everything the Lord has said; we will obey."*

To ratify the covenant, Moses sprinkled the people with blood of the sacrifice. God then commands Moses to continue up Sinai to receive the stone tablets He had prepared. Moses took Joshua with him and sent the others down to the foot of Sinai. Joshua waited while Moses continued the ascent.

For six days, a cloud covers the top of the mountain. On the seventh day, God calls Moses to enter the cloud and approach the top of the mountain. Moses stayed there for 40 days and 40 nights (Exodus 24:18). During this meeting, God gave Moses the Ten Commandments written on stone tablets by God Himself. Moses also received complete instructions on how to build the Tabernacle, the Ark of the Covenant, the Altar, and specifications for the Priestly Garments (Exodus 24–31).

Unfortunately, during this time, the people convinced Aaron to build a golden calf and were committing idolatry. When Moses and Joshua descended the mountain, Moses, in anger, broke the stone tablets and destroyed the golden calf (Exodus 32:19).

Since Aaron was God's chosen high priest and had made the idol, some believe that part of his punishment may have involved the loss of two of his adult sons (Exodus 28:1-2). Or perhaps he escaped punishment because he had already been chosen as high priest of Israel, and his role in leading worship in the tabernacle remained vital. The position of high priest was promised in Exodus 28 before Aaron molded the golden calf in Exodus 32.

In the <u>seventh ascent</u>, to intercede on behalf of the children of Israel, Moses offers his own life in exchange for the life of Israel (Exodus 32:32). God forgives and renews the covenant with Israel.

During the <u>eighth ascent</u>, God came down in the cloud and told Moses, *"Chisel out two stone tablets like the first ones, and I will write on them the words that were on the first tablets, which you broke. Be ready in the morning and then come up on Mount Sinai. Present yourself to me there on top of the mountain."*

Moses came alone, and the Lord described Himself this way: *"The Lord, the Lord, the compassionate and gracious God, slow to anger, abounding in love and faithfulness."* Moses worshiped the Lord and was on Sinai for another 40 days and 40 nights, without eating bread or drinking water.

When Moses came down the mountain, his face shone with God's glory, frightening the people. Because of this, Moses wore a veil over his face to shroud the glory. How long Moses wore the veil is unknown, but presumably, the glory faded when Moses no longer regularly went into God's presence.

The **Pentateuch** is the first five books of the Bible that most Bible scholars believe were written by Moses. The word Pentateuch comes from a combination of the Greek word *"penta,"* meaning "five," and "teuchos," which can be translated as "scroll." Therefore, it refers to the five scrolls that comprise the first of three divisions of the Jewish canon. Also known as the **Torah**, the Hebrew word meaning "<u>Law</u>," these five books of the Bible are <u>Genesis, Exodus, Leviticus, Numbers, and Deuteronomy</u>. Jesus Himself referenced the Pentateuch as the ***"Law of Moses"*** (Luke 24:44).

 **Genesis** (*Bereishit*): The beginning of creation, the fall of man, the promise of redemption, the beginning of human civilization, and the beginning of God's covenant relationship with His chosen nation, Israel.

Exodus (*Shəmot*): Records God's deliverance of His people from the bondage of Egyptian slavery and the preparation for their possession of the Promised Land. It defines the rise of Moses as their deliverer, the plagues God brought upon Egypt, and the departure from Egypt. It speaks of the wandering in the wilderness and God's Law written on stone tablets. It describes the construction of the Ark of the Covenant and the plan for the Tabernacle with its various sacrifices, altars, furniture, ceremonies, and forms of worship.

Leviticus (*Vayikra*): Takes place while the Israelites are encamped at the foot of Mt. Sinai and expands on the instructions for how Israel is to worship God and govern themselves. It lays forth the requirements of the sacrificial system that would allow God to overlook the sins of His people until the perfect and ultimate sacrifice of Jesus Christ would provide redemption and completely atone for the sins of all of God's elect. The primary theme of Leviticus is holiness. Moses was given explicit instructions on how God should be worshiped and guidelines for maintaining purity and holiness among the people.

Numbers (*Bəmidbar*): Essentially bridges the gap between the Israelites receiving the Law and preparing them to enter the Promised Land. It covers key events during the 40 years that Israel wandered in the wilderness and additional instructions for worshiping God and living as His covenant people. The theme of obedience and rebellion, followed by repentance and blessing, runs throughout the book.

Deuteronomy (*Dəvarim*): Sometimes referred to as the "*second law*" or "*repetition of the law*." It records the final words of Moses before the nation of Israel crosses over into the Promised Land (Deuteronomy 1:1). As Israel is moving into a new chapter of their history as God's chosen nation Moses reminds them not only of God's commandments and their responsibilities but of the blessings that would be theirs by obeying God and the curses that would come from disobedience. Deuteronomy shows Moses giving several sermons–type speeches to the people, reminding them of God's saving power and faithfulness. In Deuteronomy, we have a beautiful picture of a loving God who wants a relationship with His children.

Even though Moses was the leader and prophet chosen by God, he was prohibited from entering the Promised Land because of his sin at Meribah. He was, however, allowed to look upon the Promised Land. Before Moses died, God told him to climb Mount Nebo, a high mountain in Moab rising more than 4,000 feet above the Dead Sea. It is situated on the east side of the Jordan River opposite Jericho. God stated:

> "*Go up into the Abarim Range to Mount Nebo in Moab, across from Jericho, and view Canaan, the land I am giving the Israelites as their own possession. There on the mountain that you have climbed you will die and be gathered to your people, just as your brother Aaron died on Mount Hor and was gathered to his people. You will see the land only from a distance; you will not enter the land I am giving to the people of Israel*" (Deuteronomy 32:48–52).

After viewing the Promised Land from this high vantage point, Moses died, and the LORD buried him in Moab, in the valley opposite Beth Peor. However, to this day, no one knows where his grave is located. Some believe that God buried Moses in secret, without a grave marker, to prevent the site from becoming a shrine or a place of worship.

Mount Nebo is also the likely site of the conflict between Satan and the archangel Michael over Moses' body (Jude 1:9). The Book of Jude tells us that God sent Michael to deal in some way with the body of Moses. Some scholars think that Satan, ever the accuser of God's people, may have resisted the raising of Moses to eternal life on the grounds of Moses' sin at Meribah and his murder of the Egyptian (Revelation 12:10).

Some also think that the prophet Jeremiah took and hid the Ark of the Covenant, the Tent of Meeting, and the Altar of Incense in a cave on Mount Nebo and sealed the cave entrance. However, scripture says that John saw the Ark within God's temple in heaven (Revelation 11:19).

Finally, it is interesting to note that although Moses never set foot in the Promised Land during his lifetime, he may have been given that opportunity after his death. On the Mount of Transfiguration, when Jesus gave His disciples a taste of His full glory, He was accompanied by two Old Testament figures, Moses and Elijah, who represented the Law and the Prophets.

The "high mountain" that we call the Mount of Transfiguration is never clearly identified in Scripture, but some believe it is either Mount Tabor or Mount Hermon. Mount Tabor is less than 2,000 feet and is the location of the Church of the Transfiguration, which is built on the ruins of a fourth-century church.

Mount Hermon is a much taller mountain, reaching almost 10,000 feet, and is situated closer to Caesarea Philippi, where the earlier events in Matthew 16 occurred. For these reasons, some scholars believe Mount Hermon is a more plausible candidate for the Mount of Transfiguration. Despite a thorough examination, the exact location of the Mount of Transfiguration remains undetermined.

Most people do not know that Moses was a composer of songs. One was sung after crossing the Red Sea, Exodus 15, and is recorded in Psalms 90. The other was written in the last days of Moses' life in Deuteronomy 32. God told Moses to write the song, commonly called *"The Song of Moses,"* and teach it to the people, and then the Lord commissioned Joshua as Moses' replacement (Deuteronomy 31:19, 30).

Psalm 90, the oldest Psalm, was written by Moses, and is entitled "From Everlasting to Everlasting" and is noted as *"A Prayer of Moses, the man of God."* It is a prayer that contrasts God's eternity and man's mortality. It seems to have been inspired by Israel's wandering in the desert, which was punishment for their disobedience. Here, Moses focuses on God's greatness, our human weakness, and our need for the Lord to provide grace for our daily needs. We are to seek wisdom and to live each day to its fullest for the glory of God.

Some of you may have seen Michelangelo's famous statue of Moses on display in the Basilica of St. Peter in Rome. You may have wondered why the statue shows Moses with two horns on his head. When Moses came down from Mount Sinai with the two stone tablets showing the 10 Commandments, his skin glowed because he had been talking with God (Exodus 34:29). When the people saw Moses' shining face, they were afraid to go near him, so Moses covered his face with a veil.

The horn idea comes from a Latin translation. The original Hebrew word used to describe the radiant skin of Moses' face is *"qaran,"* meaning that Moses' face *"sent forth rays of light."* The Latin Vulgate translation in the fourth century used the Latin word *"cornuta"* to describe Moses' face. Cornuta, related to the word *"cornucopia,"* means *"horn of plenty."* This wording led to many literal interpretations by artists who assumed that

Moses had horns protruding from his face when he descended Mount Sinai.

The **Septuagint** is the Ancient Greek translation of the Hebrew Bible and refers to the face of Moses as *"glorified."* The apostle Paul confirms that this is indeed the correct meaning:

"Now if the ministry that brought death, which was engraved in letters on stone, came with glory, so that the Israelites could not look steadily at the face of Moses because of its glory" (2 Corinthians 3:7).

"**Moses seat**": As recorded in Matthew 23, Moses would sit here from morning to evening to serve as judge for the people. A "seat" in this context is a place of authority and is similar to our modern word "bench." A judge may be said to "occupy the bench." In Jesus' day, the teachers of the law and Pharisees continued in the footsteps of Moses in that they were the interpreters and enforcers of the law. In that way, they are said to "sit in Moses' seat."

If someone wanted to know what Moses would say about something, he would consult an expert in the Law of Moses—a Pharisee or a teacher of the law. However, Jesus points out that even though what these leaders say may be correct, they do not practice what they preach. Jesus pronounced seven woes against the Jewish religious leaders. He said  to His disciples and the crowd around them, *"The teachers of the law and the Pharisees sit in Moses' seat. So you must be careful to do everything they tell you. But do not do what they do, for they do not practice what they preach"* (Exodus 18:13).

One of the most asked questions is: *If Moses met face to face with God, then why was he later not allowed to see God's face?* Before the official tabernacle, a tent would be pitched outside the camp, and Moses would use this tent to intercede for the people of Israel. <u>A pillar of cloud would come down and stay at the entrance, while the Lord spoke with Moses</u>. Exodus 33:11 states that the Lord spoke "face to face" with Moses, but it does not say that Moses <u>saw</u> God face to face. God said, "**You cannot see My face; for no man shall see Me, and live**" (Exodus 33:20).

When Moses entered the tent, the pillar of cloud descended and stood at the tent's entrance, and the LORD spoke with Moses. The Lord's presence was visible, not in human form but as Yahweh standing in front of it in the glory cloud.

At one point Moses asked the Lord, "*Please show me your glory.*" In response, the Lord told Moses, "*I will make all my goodness pass before you, but you cannot see my face, for man shall not see me and live. While my glory passes by, I will put you in a cleft of the rock, and I will cover you with my hand until I have passed by. Then I will take away my hand, and you will see my back, but my face shall not be seen.*"

In the Book of Numbers, we see the term "face to face" when Moses interceded with the Lord, pleading for him not to punish Israel for their threatened rebellion. Moses says to God, "*For you, O LORD, are seen face to face, and your cloud stands over them and you go before them, in a pillar of cloud by day and in a pillar of fire by night*" (Numbers. 14:14). Israel saw the LORD "face to face" but it was actually in the manifestation of the pillar of cloud and the pillar of fire. Moses reminded the Israelites that when they were at the foot of Horeb, they had seen no "form" at all but only heard a voice emanating from the mountain (Deuteronomy 4:12).

Scripture does not teach that God is a literal man who appeared to Moses in an embodied form. To the contrary, in every passage referring to Moses or Israel coming "face to face" with the Lord, his divine presence is seen in a cloud or fire, not in a human body (Exodus 33:11).

Reading this makes Jesus' words to Philip all the more amazing: "*Anyone who has seen me has seen the Father*" (John 14:9). When Jesus walked this earth with His glory veiled, we could look Him in the face. *"In Christ all the fullness of the Deity lives in bodily form"* (Colossians 2:9).

This verse reminds us that Jesus is not only fully human but also fully divine and that he embodies God's nature. On one brief occasion, Jesus' glory was revealed in this world, and this was at the Transfiguration.

"And he was transfigured before them, and his face shone like the sun, and his clothes became white as light" (Matthew 17:2-3). Interestingly, Moses was there, speaking to the glorified Lord, face to face.

Moses was a Hebrew prophet, teacher, and leader whom God specifically chose to deliver His people from Egyptian slavery. After 40 years of wandering in the desert, Moses died on Mount Nebo when he was 120 years old and within sight of the Promised Land. The religions of Judaism, Christianity, and Islam claim him. Interestingly, Muhammad is referred to by name only four times in the Quran, but Moses is mentioned 136 times.

The Dispute with Satan Over Moses' Body

I recently finished a study of Moses and followed it up with one on Joshua, Moses' loyal assistant, who took the Israelites over into the Promised Land. But before we leave Moses completely, let's discuss a time after Moses died when Satan wanted to claim the body of Moses.

Scripture tells us that Moses was born in Egypt to Hebrew parents but became the adopted son of Pharaoh's daughter. As he grew older, he saw that the people of Israel suffered greatly, and after killing an Egyptian who was beating one of the Israelites, he fled west and settled in the land of Midian. Here, as a shepherd, he met God as a burning bush. God instructed Moses to return to Egypt and lead the Israelites out of slavery and into the Promised Land. At Mount Sinai, Moses received the two stone tablets that were the Ten Commandments.

Moses was not allowed to enter the Promised Land because, at one point, he was told to speak to a rock that would bring forth water for the thirsty Israelites. Moses, however, struck the rock twice with his staff. This showed a lack of faith and respect for God, and Moses was barred from entering the Promised Land. But God did take Moses to the top of Mt. Nebo and showed him all the land designated to the descendants of Abraham, Isaac, and Jacob—the *Promised Land*.

"So Moses the servant of the Lord died there in the land of Moab, according to the word of the Lord. And he buried him in a valley in the land of Moab, over against Bethpeor: but no man knoweth of his sepulchre unto this day" (Deuteronomy 34:5-6).

This is unique in Scripture, as it seems to be the only instance where God is directly involved in a burial. It underscores the special relationship between God and Moses.

The specific location of Moses' burial, "*over against Bethpeor*," also holds symbolic meaning. It was a place associated with the worship of foreign gods, highlighting the contrast between the Moabites' pagan practices and the Israelites' monotheistic faith.

The "sepulcher" (sep-ul-chur) is a burial place, such as a grave, cave, or tomb. Death is life's shadow, and all that lives is destined to die. Moses was 120 years old when he died, and "his eye was not dim, nor his natural force abated."

The mysterious nature of Moses' burial leads to many speculations. The Jewish works The Assumption of Moses and The Testament of Moses also mention events about Moses' death, but much of the text of these writings is incomplete or has been lost.

Scripture reminds us that spiritual battles are constantly being waged over the souls of men and nations. Satan is described as an angelic enemy of God and all who follow God. Michael the Archangel is described as a warrior angel who engages in spiritual combat. The word archangel means *"angel of the highest rank."*

Jude (Judas in some translations) is the author of the Epistle of Jude and one of Jesus' four brothers—James, Joset, and Simon (Matthew 13:55, Mark 6:3). In this epistle (letter), we are told of a confrontation between Michael and Satan. The details of Moses' death are limited, but it is known that God sent Michael the Archangel to deal with Moses' body.

"But even the archangel Michael, when he was disputing with the devil about the body of Moses, did not himself dare to condemn him for slander but said, "The Lord rebuke you!" (Jude 1:9).

The term "**rebuke**" biblically means to reprimand, strongly warn, or restrain those who deviate from God's commandments. *"The Lord rebuke you"* highlights God's protection of His chosen people and his divine authority. Michael's humility acknowledges that the power to confront and rebuke Satan comes from God and emphasizes that ALL authority belongs to God. Even the most powerful angels, like Satan, do not operate outside of His sovereignty.

As we each face spiritual warfare, we should never forget that victory comes through the strength of the Lord, not our strength.

"The Lord is my strength and my shield; in him my heart trusts, and I am helped; my heart exults, and with my song I give thanks to him" (Psalms 28:7).

So, why did Satan want the body of Moses?
There are many theories, so let's look at a few:

(A) A possible explanation lies in the importance of Moses. He was one of the most prominent prophets in the Old Testament and best remembered for leading the Israelites out of Egypt to the Promised Land. Additionally, he is credited with writing the first five books of the Bible (*the Pentateuch*). Because of the important part that Moses played in God's plan, Satan may have wanted to defile or misuse the body of Moses. Michael was defending one of God's people against any of Satan's evil plans.

(B) Perhaps Satan thought that the Israelites might build an altar to Moses and worship him. That would be idolatry. Satan would love for people to worship things other than God. Moses held an exalted position in the eyes of the people and was the only leader the Israelites ever had. It's quite possible they would have wanted to carry the body of Moses with them into the land of Canaan (as they did that of Joseph), bury him, and erect an elaborate shrine over his remains.

(C) Satan may have resisted the raising of Moses to eternal life based on Moses' sin at the *Rock of Meri bah* and his murder of the Egyptian (Exodus 2:12). Perhaps Satan wanted to claim not only Moses' body, but also his soul. Satan is also called the accuser of the brethren, and in Zechariah 3, we see something similar. Joshua, the High Priest of Israel, stands before the angel of the Lord with Satan accusing him. Joshua is cleared of guilt and clothed with new garments, replacing his guilt with the Lord's justifying righteousness.

(D) Some think Satan wanted the body of Moses to receive his Glory. We are reminded that Moses met with God on Mount Sinai and received the 10 Commandments. Moses came down from the mountain with a shining face of God's glory (Exodus 34:29).

(E) Perhaps Satan wanted Moses's body to duplicate it or take on the form of his looks so he could deceive many by making them think he was appearing to them. Satan might try to use Moses' body as the anti-Christ person after the Rapture of the church to gain the complete following of the Jews.

Only God knows the actual reason that Satan wanted the body. Since scripture does not tell us all of the details concerning the Michael/Satan event, the theories offered as to why Satan wanted to have Moses' body are only speculation.

God doesn't always explain the mysteries, so I guess we will have to wait and discuss this with Moses in heaven before we know the entire story.

Remember that Moses, the great leader who led the Israelites out of Egypt and received the Ten Commandments on Mount Sinai, had a special relationship with God. Satan, as the adversary and accuser in the Bible, is actively working to oppose God's plans and disrupt His purposes.

Satan may have contested Moses' death to challenge God's authority over life and death. By demanding Moses' body, Satan may have been trying to assert his control over life, challenging God's sovereign will to hide Moses' grave. This challenge could be seen as another attempt by Satan to interfere in God's redemptive plan, just as he did when he tempted Adam and Eve or tried to stop Jesus from fulfilling His mission.

The Life and Times of Joshua

The Book of Joshua emphasizes God's faithfulness, the importance of obedience, and the necessity of faith and courage to meet life's many challenges. It also provides an overview of the military campaigns to conquer the land God had promised to the descendants of Abraham. Joshua wrote the book, although some think there were possible contributions from Aaron's son Eleazar the priest and/or Phinehas, his son. The Book of Joshua was likely written between 1400 and 1370 B.C.

Joshua was born in Egypt, the son of Nun, into the tribe of Ephraim, one of the Twelve Tribes of Israel. His birth name, Hoshea, means "salvation," and it is cognate to the name Joshua, which is generally more popular. Joshua, in Hebrew, means "the Lord is my salvation." Not much is recorded about Joshua's immediate family other than that he was one of the enslaved Israelites in Egypt.

A bit of history: A seven-year famine was responsible for God's chosen people ending up in Egypt. Initially, the people flourished under the leadership of Joseph, who was second in charge of the country after Pharaoh. But things changed, and for several centuries the Israelites were enslaved by the Egyptians who *"worked them ruthlessly"* (Exodus 1:13).

Moses and Aaron (Moses' older brother), were sent by God to rescue the people. After enduring the last of the ten plagues, the death of the Egyptian firstborn males, Pharaoh agreed to release the people. However, a bit later, he decided to pursue and kill the fleeing Israelites.  The parting of the Red Sea is a foundational story in the Bible and tells of Moses parting the water. The Lord then caused a strong east wind to blow, turning the sea floor into dry land. Once the Israelites were safely on the other side, the sea closed over the top of the pursuing Egyptians, killing them all.

The Israelites' exodus from Egypt marked the end of a period of oppression for Abraham's descendants and the beginning of the fulfillment of the covenant promise to Abraham that his descendants would not only live in the Promised Land but also multiply and become a great nation (Genesis 12:1-3).

<u>**Moses' interaction with Joshua**</u>: Joshua learned from Moses and saw many miracles that God did through Moses. He also witnessed many of Moses' hardships and his anger and frustration at times with the people of Israel. For forty-plus years, Joshua learned leadership and what it was to care for the people, pray for them, intercede for them, and offer sacrifices for them. Joshua knew how to lead because he had seen Moses do it for decades.

He knew about the importance of approaching God correctly, appropriately, reverently, and according to the way God has specifically prescribed. Joshua was Moses' loyal assistant, and, alongside **Caleb**, he stood faithful to God when other Israelites rebelled. In the Book of Exodus, we see that Moses and Joshua went up on Mount Sinai, but only Moses went to the top to meet God. Joshua was a servant of Moses and God from his youth.

We are now basically where our story of Joshua begins. While in *Rephidim (raf-a-dem),* a place where the Israelites rested in their journey going from Egypt to Sinai, the *Amalekites (a-mal-a-kites)*, a mighty and fierce people, descendants of Esau and well-trained in the art of warfare, suddenly attacked the people of Israel. It was an unprovoked attack upon a tired and weary group just liberated from slavery and on the way to a new life.

Moses told Joshua to lead a select group of warriors to fight against them. Moses would stand on a hill above the battle with the "*staff of God*" in hand, which represented God's power.

Joshua went to battle, and Moses, Aaron, and Hur, a member of the tribe of Judah, climbed to the top of the hill. Whenever Moses held up his hands, the Israelites prevailed, but whenever he put his hands down, the Amalekites started

winning. When Moses got tired, Aaron and Hur held his arms up. Joshua defeated the Amalekites, and Moses built an altar called "The Lord is My Banner" (Exodus 17:8-18).

Upon arriving at Kadesh Barnea, which bordered the Promised Land of Canaan, Moses sent twelve spies to survey the land and its people (Numbers 13:18-25). They returned after forty days of exploration, and ten of the spies reported that they could not attack because the people were descendants of Anak, who were giants, and the cities were fortified and very large. However, **Joshua**, the son of Nun, and **Caleb**, the son of Jephunneh, were two spies who said the land was exceedingly good and that they should trust God's will and go forward.

The people believed the ten who gave the bad report and lost heart of going into the land. God was not pleased that the people did not trust Him and decided that only their children, Caleb and Joshua, would enter the Promised Land. The people would instead suffer by wandering in the wilderness for *forty years, one year for each of the forty days they explored the land* (Numbers 14:34). Additionally, the ten men who had given the bad report were struck down and died of a plague. God had promised the people the land, and all they had to do was trust God and go in and take it.

"*Without faith it is impossible to please God*" (Hebrews 11:6).

Moses was also not allowed to enter the Promised Land. Nearing the end of their forty years of wandering, the Israelites came to the *Desert of Zin* without water. The people once again rebelled against Moses and Aaron.

God told Moses to gather the disgruntled assembly, speak to the rock, and water would then come forth. Instead of speaking to the rock as God instructed, Moses, seemingly in anger, struck the rock twice with his staff (Numbers 20:10-11). Water came from the rock as God had promised, but Moses had not done what God had instructed.

However, God was faithful to His promise and later took Moses to Mount Nebo, where He showed His beloved prophet the Promised Land before Moses died at 120 years old (Deuteronomy 34:4-5).

After Moses' death, God appointed Joshua as the new leader of the Israelites and commissioned him to lead the people across the *Jordan River* to conquer and take possession of the Promised Land. Joshua was about 80 years of age. God assured Joshua that He would be with him and urged Joshua to be strong and courageous in fulfilling this task. Joshua then instructed the Israelite people to prepare to cross the Jordan River and take possession of the land.

Before crossing the Jordan River, Joshua told the people they were to follow the **Ark of the Covenant** at a distance of two thousand cubits (3000 feet). The Ark represented God's presence and support for the people. When the priests carrying the Ark stepped into the river, upstream flooding water was held back, creating a dry path for the Israelites to cross. The priests who carried the Ark stopped in the middle of the Jordan and stood on the dry ground, while all Israel passed by until the whole nation had completed the crossing.

Then Joshua chose twelve men, one from each tribe, and told them to take up twelve stones from the middle of the Jordan and take them to their camp. These stones would later serve forever as a memorial to the people of Israel that the flow of the Jordan River was cut off before the Ark of the Covenant of the Lord.

The water returned to normal after the Israelites were safely on the west side of the river. About forty thousand soldiers were armed for battle and crossed over to the plains of Jericho for war. The people went from the Jordan and camped at *Gilgal* on the eastern border of Jericho. Here, Joshua set up the twelve stones they had taken out of the Jordan River as a memorial to God.

The Israelites prepared to enter the Promised Land by renewing their covenant with God through a mass circumcision. God instructed Joshua to circumcise all the men of Israel who were born in the wilderness, signifying a fresh commitment to the covenant.

The Israelites who disobeyed God had roamed in the wilderness for forty years until all the men who were of military age when they left Egypt had died. The sons were raised in their place, and these were the ones Joshua circumcised. They stayed in camp until they were healed. The group then celebrated Passover and no longer depended on the manna from heaven for food.

Jericho: The name means fragrance; the city is called the "*City of Palms.*" It is thought to be one of the oldest cities in the world, and is situated at the foot of the Judean Mountains, about eight miles northwest of where the Jordan flows into the Dead Sea. This city was of strategic military importance because it was located at the eastern entrance into Palestine. Its conquest was the key that would unlock the door to the rest of the Jordan Valley.

As the group neared Jericho, Joshua saw a man standing before him with a drawn sword. Joshua went up to him and asked, *"Are you for us or for our enemies?"* The man replied, "Neither," and stated he was *"Commander of the Army of the Lord."* Joshua was told to, *"Take off your sandals, for the place where you are standing is holy."* The divine messenger was there to affirm God's presence and support for the Israelites as they began the conquest of Canaan (Joshua 5:13).

The Commander of the Army of the Lord could be an example of a *theophany* *(the-op-any)*— a theological term referring to temporary, visible manifestations of God. Joshua was to take off his sandals like Moses did at the burning bush when he met God (Exodus 3:5).

Some think the commander was an angel since no one can see God and live (Exodus 33:20). Or perhaps this was God the Son, a pre-incarnate appearance of Jesus Christ. Whether the Commander of the Lord's army was angelic or divine, God communicated a vital message to Joshua to prepare him for the upcoming battle.

The City of Jericho was a secure fortress with high, formidable walls, and Joshua sent two spies into the city to gather information before the Israelite invasion. The spies were seen and sought refuge in the house of a Canaanite prostitute named **Rahab.** She hid them on the rooftop of her home away from the king of Jericho and his men. She was aware of recent events, such as the Exodus and the Red Sea miracle, and was convinced that it was God's will for Israel to capture Jericho.

She believed in the God of Israel and acknowledged the miracles He had performed. She then secured a promise from the spies to protect her and her family when the city was conquered. Rahab was instructed to hang a scarlet rope from her window as a sign for the Israelites to protect her family. Rahab then let the men down from the outside wall using the scarlet rope and directed the spies westward to safety in the plains of Jordan.

Before the battle of Jericho, God gave Joshua specific instructions. The men of war were to march in silence around the city once each day for six days. The priests were to walk with them, blowing ram's horns and carrying the ark of the covenant as a sign of God's presence among them.

On the seventh day, they were to march around the city seven times. The priests were to blow their trumpets at the appropriate signal, and the people would shout a mighty shout. They did exactly as God had commanded, and on the seventh day the walls of Jericho crumbled. Joshua's soldiers went in and took the city, destroying it completely. Only Rahab and her family were spared.

Joshua pronounced a curse on the city:

"Cursed before the Lord be the man who rises up and rebuilds this city, Jericho. At the cost of his firstborn shall he lay its foundation, and at the cost of his youngest son shall he set up its gates" (Joshua 6:26).

Joshua's curse did come true later when **Hiel of Bethel** rebuilt Jericho. He did so at a significant personal cost—the loss of his sons Abiram and Segub. Joshua did not promise Jericho would never be rebuilt; he said that the person who rebuilt it would be judged by the loss of his firstborn son and youngest son (1 Kings 16:34).

Jericho was the first city to fall in the conquest of Canaan, and the victory was dedicated to the Lord (Joshua 6:17). The people of Israel were to take no spoils of war. Joshua commanded that *"all the silver and gold and the articles of bronze and iron are sacred to the Lord and must go into his treasury."* Jericho would serve as a "tithe" to the Lord, who gave them victory.

The Israelites met defeat at a place called **Ai** (*eye*), a Canaanite town located approximately two miles east of *Bethel*. Joshua had sent spies to the city, and they returned, saying that the city was weak and that not all of Joshua's army would be needed for the attack. The small town of Ai routed the Israelite army of about 3000 men and inflicted three dozen casualties. Joshua was devastated and cried to the Lord, *"Why did you allow this to happen?"*

> God said, *"Israel has sinned; they have violated my covenant, which I commanded them to keep. They have taken some of the devoted things; they have stolen, they have lied, they have put them with their own possessions."*

The defeat was due to **Achan's** sin. In direct defiance of

God's command to keep nothing for themselves from the wicked city of Jericho, Achan had kept a robe, two hundred shekels of silver, and a fifty-shekel bar of gold, and hid it all in a hole he had dug within his tent (Joshua 7:1-5). Achan kept his theft a secret, and God revealed the cause for this defeat to Joshua. Achan, his family, and everything he owned were destroyed at the Valley of Achor (Joshua 7:25-26).

Joshua and the entire army moved out to once again attack Ai. He chose thirty thousand of his best fighting men and sent them out at night with the orders to set an ambush behind the

city. When Joshua and the rest of his army marched on the town, the Ai men came out against them, and as they did, Joshua and his army pretended to flee. While the

Ai army chased them, Joshua's army rose from the ambush, took the city, and set it on fire.

Twelve thousand men and women fell that day—all the people of Ai. The Israelite warriors captured the king and brought him to Joshua, who impaled him and left his body on public display as a testament to Israel's great triumph over the enemies of the Lord. The body of the king of Ai was left impaled until evening, at which time it was thrown through the gate of Ai's entrance and piled over with rocks.

After experiencing a terrible defeat at Ai due to hidden sin, Israel learned about the importance of purging sin from their midst so that the Lord could fight for them. This also demonstrates how one person's sin can affect everyone around them.

Joshua then built an altar to the Lord, the God of Israel, on Mount Ebal. It was constructed according to what is written in the Book of the Law of Moses: an altar of uncut stones, on which no iron tool had been used. They then offered the Lord burnt offerings and sacrificed fellowship offerings. Afterward, Joshua read all the words of the law, including the blessings and the curses, just as it is written in the Book of the Law.

It was now that all the Amorite kings west of the Jordan came together to wage war against Joshua and Israel. But a group called the **Gibeonites**, descended from the Amorites, tried to deceive the Israelites to protect themselves.

The Gibeonites went as a delegation, their donkeys loaded with worn-out sacks and old wineskins, cracked and mended. They put worn and patched sandals on their feet and wore old clothes. All the bread in their food supply was dry and moldy. They went to Joshua in the Gilgal camp and said they were from a distant country and wanted to make a treaty with the Israelites.

The Israelites agreed to the treaty, but the big problem was that they did not consult God before the agreement. It wasn't long before the Israelites discovered they had been tricked and discussed how to respond. The leaders of Israel decided:

"We have given them our oath by the Lord, the God of Israel, and we cannot touch them now. This is what we will do to them: We will let them live, so that God's wrath will not fall on us for breaking the oath we swore to them."

The leader's promise was kept, and they let the Gibeonites live, but made them be woodcutters and water carriers in the service of the whole assembly. The Gibeonites served as slaves to the Israelites for generations to come. The land of Gibeon would later be allotted to the tribe of Benjamin (Joshua 21:17).

Fast Forward in Time: **King Saul** was the son of Kish from the tribe of Benjamin. Saul was 30 years old, came from a wealthy family, and was tall, dark, and handsome (1 Samuel 9:1). He was God's chosen one to lead the scattered nation of Israel, a collection of tribes that did not have a central leader or formal government. These were turbulent times of war, and the people  pressed the prophet **Samuel** to appoint a king to rule them (1 Samuel 8:5). God allowed it because the people had rejected God as king and served other gods.

Saul's 42-year reign over Israel started peacefully, but the peace did not last long. Saul made a series of serious blunders that began his downfall as king. God eventually withdrew His Spirit from Saul. While Saul would be allowed to serve the rest of his life as king, he was plagued by an evil spirit that tormented him and brought about waves of madness (1 Samuel 16:14-23).

At one point, King Saul broke the treaty Joshua had previously signed and attacked the Gibeonites. Later, during the time of King David, famine occurred in Israel. When David asked the Lord about the famine, God said, *"It is on account of Saul and his blood-stained house; it is because he put the Gibeonites to death"* (2 Samuel 21:1). To appease the Gibeonites and put an end to the famine, seven descendants of

Saul were given to them to be put to death. God healed Israel's land after that (2 Samuel 21:14).

Adoni-Zedek, king of Jerusalem, heard that Joshua had not only taken Jericho and Ai, but that the people of Gibeon had made a treaty of peace with Israel and had become their allies. The king of Jerusalem appealed to **Hoham**, *king of Hebron*, **Piram**, *king of Jarmuth*, **Japhia**, *king of Lachish, and* **Debir**, *king of Eglon*, and asked for help in attacking Gibeon. Canaan was now not a nation but a land where kings ruled over cities and territories. The five Amorite kings joined forces and attacked Gibeon.

The Gibeonites then sent word to Joshua asking for help. Joshua made an all-night march up from Gilgal with his entire army, and God told Joshua, *"Do not be afraid of them; I have given them into your hand. Not one of them will be able to withstand you."* Joshua took them by surprise, and the Israelites routed them at Gibeon. Those fleeing from the Israelites were killed by large stones hurled by the Lord (Joshua 10:10-11).

This battle tells of another extraordinary miracle God performed—He made the sun and moon stand still. Joshua said to the Lord in the presence of Israel: **"Sun, stand still over Gibeon, and you, moon, over the Valley of Aijalon."** The sun stopped in the middle of the sky and delayed going down by about a whole day. God miraculously provided twenty-four hours of light to aid Israel in destroying their enemy, the Amorites (Joshua 10:12-14). Joshua prayed, and God supernaturally allowed Joshua to win the battle.

The five Amorite kings had fled and hid in the cave at *Makkedah*. They were discovered, and large rocks were rolled up to the mouth of the cave while the Israelite army pursued the army. Joshua and his army defeated the Amorites completely. Joshua then had the five kings brought out of the cave and told the army commanders to put their feet on the necks of the kings, and they did. Then Joshua put the kings to death and left their bodies hanging on the poles until evening. At sunset, Joshua gave the order to take the kings down and throw their bodies into the cave where they had been hiding. Large rocks were placed at the mouth of the cave.

That day Joshua took the city of **Makkedah**, put its king to the sword, and left no survivors. Joshua and his army moved from Makkedah to **Libnah**, leaving no survivors. The army then took the city of **Lachish** and later defeated Horam, *king of* **Gezer**, and his army. Then Joshua took **Eglon**, **Hebron**, and **Debir**. Joshua subdued the whole region and left no survivors. He destroyed all who breathed, <u>just as the God of Israel had commanded</u>. Joshua subdued them from **Kadesh Barnea to Gaza** and Goshen to the Gibeon region. Joshua conquered all these kings and their lands in one campaign because the God of Israel favored them. Then Joshua returned with all Israel to the camp at Gilgal.

When God called his people out of slavery in Egypt and sent them into this land, He told Moses and Joshua that they were to kill ALL the Canaanite clans who were living in the land (Deuteronomy 7:1). This would include the Hittites, Girgashites, Amorites, Canaanites, Perizzites, Hivites, and Jebusites.

In Genesis 9:25, God cursed the Canaanites from their very beginning. They were evil people who practiced the basest forms of immorality. If their evil continued, it could completely contaminate the rest of society. The Lord God of Israel is holy and cannot allow sin to go unpunished. In His patience, He had spared the people of Canaan for centuries, but He spared them no longer.

The Northern kings were composed of **Jabin**, *king of Hazor, Jobab, king of Madon,* **Shimron**, **Akshaph**, **Arabah**, **Naphoth Dor**, *the* **Canaanites**, **Amorites**, **Hittites**, **Perizzites**, **Jebusites**, *and the* **Hivites**. They formed a massive army, as numerous as the sand on the seashore. All these kings joined forces and camped at the *Waters of Merom* to fight against Israel.

But the Lord told Joshua, *"Do not be afraid of them, because by this time tomorrow I will hand all of them, slain, over to Israel. You are to hamstring their horses and burn their chariots."*

Joshua and his army came against them, and the armies of the Northern kings were defeated. Joshua did as the Lord had directed them, and he hamstrung their horses and burned their chariots. Joshua then captured the city of **Hazor**. The Israelites took plunder and livestock from all the cities. And all the people were put to the sword... as the Lord had commanded Moses and Joshua.

Joshua took the land, captured all 31 kings, and killed them. Except for the *Hivites* living in Gibeon, no other city made a peace treaty with the Israelites. For it was the Lord himself who hardened their hearts to wage war against Israel, so that he might destroy them totally, exterminating them without mercy. Joshua took the entire land and would give it as an inheritance to Israel according to their tribal divisions. Then, for a time, the land rested from war.

Joshua is now getting old, and he and Caleb are the only ones at Mount Sinai who are still alive. Joshua had been a man of war from his youth, but now age is catching up. Much land still needs to be possessed, but God is pleased with Joshua's actions. Yahweh tells Joshua to divide the land taken by the Israelite tribes.

The tribe of **Levi** didn't receive a portion of land because they were dedicated to God's service and received a portion of the sacrifices offered in the Tabernacle. The tribes of **Reuben**, **Gad**, and half the tribe of **Manasseh** received land on the east side of the Jordan River.

Caleb approached Joshua and asked him to fulfill Moses's promise 45 years earlier. Moses promised Caleb that the land he visited on his spying mission would belong to him and his children. This was hill country where the strong Anakin people lived and had great fortified cities. Caleb told Joshua he was as strong at 85 as he was at 40, and asked Joshua to give him the land. Caleb believed the Lord would help him overcome the Anakin people.

The request was granted, and **Caleb received Hebron**, which was formerly named *Kiriath-Arba*. Caleb wasn't interested in a life of ease; he wanted to see God's power at work in his later years, as he saw it working in his younger years. The remainder of the chapter describes the lands given to the Israelites.

Five tribes (**Reuben, Gad, Manasseh, Ephraim, and Judah**) had already been promised particular pieces of land. Joshua gave them what had been promised, and they took possession and lived there. The whole assembly of the Israelites gathered at Shiloh for a meeting. There were still seven Israelite tribes who had not yet received their inheritance. Joshua then sent scouts to explore and divide the land into seven portions for the remaining seven tribes. Joshua then allotted land territories to **Benjamin, Simeon, Zebulun, Issachar, Asher, Naphtali, and Dan**.

When they had finished dividing the land into its allotted portions, the Israelites gave **Joshua** an inheritance among them, as the Lord had commanded. They gave him the town he asked for: ***Timnath Serah in the hill country of Ephraim***, and he settled there.

God then instructed the people to designate *six cities of refuge* for those who kill by mistake or unintentionally, so they may flee there and find protection from the avenger. They are to stand at the city gate's entrance and state their case before the city's elders. Then the elders are to admit the fugitive into their city and provide a place to live among them. The fugitives must stay in that city until they have stood trial. The cities of **Kedesh, Shechem, Kiriath Arba, Bezer, Ramoth**, and **Golan** were designated cities.

The family heads of the **Levites** approached Eleazar the priest, Joshua, and the heads of the other tribal families of Israel at Shiloh. They said, *"The Lord commanded through Moses that you give us towns to live in, with pasturelands for our livestock."* So, as the Lord had commanded, the Israelites gave the Levites towns and pasturelands out of their own inheritance. The cities of the Levites in the territory held by the Israelites were 48 in all, including the six refuge cities and their pasturelands.

The Lord gave Israel all the land he had sworn to give their ancestors, and they took possession of it and settled there. Every one of the Lord's promises to Israel was fulfilled. **"Not one word of all the good promises that the Lord had made to the house of Israel had failed; all came to pass"** (Joshua 21:45).

Joshua then summoned the **Reubenites, Gadites, and the half-tribe of Manasseh.** He thanked them for doing all the Lord commanded and obeying Joshua in everything he had commanded. They were told to return home and keep God's commandments. Joshua then blessed them and sent them away to their homes. All of them had great wealth and plunder from their enemies. Joshua said to share the large herds of livestock, silver, gold, bronze, iron, and the great quantity of clothing with their fellow Israelites.

The Reubenites, Gadites, and Manasseh's settled on the eastern side of the Jordan River. This land, known for its fertile pastures, was granted to them by Moses before the Israelites crossed into the Promised Land. Returning home, they came to *Geliloth* and built a large altar by the Jordan River. When the Israelites heard that they had built an altar on the Israelite side, the army of Israel gathered at Shiloh to go to war against them.

When God revealed the Law of Moses, He prohibited the building of altars other than those He had commanded (Deuteronomy 12:1-14). However, after Jacob had further discussed the issue, it was found that the altar had been built to honor God, the Lord. The Israelites were relieved to learn the altar was a memorial, not for sacrifices.

Time passed, and Joshua summoned the Israel elders, leaders, judges, and officials, and praised them for all they had done. He reminded them that God had fought for them and allowed them to have the land they inherited. He told them to be strong and obey all that is written in the Book of the Law of Moses.

He reminded them not to associate with the nations that remained among them, and not to invoke the names of their gods, swear by them, serve them, or bow down to them. Do not ally yourselves with the survivors of these nations that remain among them, and do not intermarry with them or practice idolatry.

> Joshua said, "***if they violate the covenant of the Lord, the Lord's anger will burn against you, and you will quickly perish from the good land he has given you.***"

At Shechem, Joshua recounted Israel's history and renewed the covenant with the people. After recording these things in the Book of the Law of God, he took a large stone as a witness and set it up at the oak near the holy place of the Lord. And the people said to Joshua, "*We will serve the Lord our God and obey him.*"

Joshua urged the people to forsake their idols and remain faithful to the covenant that God made with them at Sinai, saying:

> "*And if it is evil in your eyes to serve the LORD, choose this day whom you will serve, whether the gods your fathers served in the region beyond the River, or the gods of the Amorites in whose land you dwell.* **But as for me and my house, we will serve the LORD**" (Joshua 24:15).

Then Joshua dismissed the people, each to their inheritance.

Joshua, son of Nun, the servant of the Lord, died at the age of 110, and was buried in the land of his inheritance, at *Timnath Serah* in the hill country of Ephraim, north of Mount Gaash.

David, the King of Israel

The young boy named **David** had a rich and fascinating life. You do not often find a poor shepherd boy who becomes the King of Israel. His story is long (1st and 2nd Samuel, 1st Chronicles, and 1st Kings), but I hope to capture the essential parts as I mainly reference the Books of Samuel. As we go through David's life, we will also look at a few very interesting people.

The book of Ruth beautifully captures the story of David's great-grandparents, **Boaz & Ruth**. Boaz was a wealthy landowner in Bethlehem, and Ruth was a widow Moabite woman that had come to Israel with her mother-in-law, **Naomi**. Boaz and Ruth were married and had a son named **Obed,** who would later become the grandfather of King David. David's parents were **Jesse and Nitzevet**. Jesse was a farmer and sheep breeder in Bethlehem and of the Israelite tribe of Judah. David's mother, Nitzevet bat Adael, was a woman of tremendous faith and love. She was born in Bethlehem and was the daughter of Eliam, a soldier from the family of Benjamin.

According to the genealogy described in the Hebrew Bible, David was the youngest of eight sons. His brothers' names, in birth order, were **Eliab, Abinadab, Shimea, Nethanel, Raddai, Ozem, and David**. He also had two sisters named **Zeruiah and Abigail**. Only seven sons are listed, and most Bible scholars think that one of David's seven brothers must have died at a young age and was not accounted for in the later genealogical register.

As a young boy, David was a shepherd and tended to his father Jesse's sheep. He was also very good at playing the harp (lyre), which would eventually benefit him greatly.

But before we go any further, let me introduce you to the Apostle Samuel and King Saul because they play a very important part in David's story.

Samuel was a prophet, priest, judge, and military leader. His mother, Hannah, was a woman who was barren but desperately wanted a child. If you were barren, you were looked upon as an outcast and abandoned by the Lord. Despite years of disappointment, Hannah continued to pray and believe that God would bless her with a baby. God answered her prayer, and she and her husband, Elkanah, gave birth to Samuel, which means "*God has heard.*" The parents dedicated Samuel to God and entrusted his upbringing to the priest **Eli** in the temple.

Samuel served at the tabernacle, and his faithfulness and favor with God were apparent. The young boy grew in wisdom, became a prophet, and received divine messages and guidance from God. The priest Eli's sons, *Hophni* and *Phinehas* were scoundrels, had no regard for the Lord, and acted in wicked ways. They later took the *Ark of the Covenant* out to battle against the Philistines. The Israelites lost thirty thousand foot soldiers, the Ark of the Covenant was captured, and Eli's two sons, Hophni and Phinehas, died. When Eli heard the news, he fell backward from his seat, broke his neck, and died on the same day. The pregnant wife of Phinehas heard the news, went into labor, and died while giving birth. The son was named Ichabod, a name meaning "*no glory.*"

Samuel became the spiritual leader and rallied the Israelites against the Philistines at Mizpah. His leadership strengthened the people, and as a judge, he traveled to various cities, settling disputes and maintaining order.

1 Samuel 4 states that these were difficult times, and war broke out regularly between the Philistines and Israel. Because of the constant threat of war and a desire to be like the surrounding nations, the Israelites pressed Samuel to appoint a king to rule over them. Samuel disapproved of this request; however, God allowed it. The people had rejected God as king, forsaken Him, and served other gods.

God told Samuel to anoint a king as the people had asked, but also to warn them and show them the ways of the king who shall reign over them. So, it became Samuel's task to anoint a king from among the people.

King Saul: Saul came from Gibeah and was the son of **Kish**, of the family of the Marites. He was a member of the tribe of Benjamin, one of the twelve Tribes of Israel. Saul married **Ahinoam**, daughter of *Ahimaaz*, with whom he sired at least five sons (***Jonathan, Abinadab, Malchishua, Ishvi***, and **Ish-bosheth**) and two daughters (***Merab*** and ***Michal***).

The Hebrew name "Saul" means "*asked for, prayed for.*" Saul came from a wealthy family and was tall, dark, and handsome. He was God's chosen one to lead the scattered nation of Israel, which at that time was simply a collection of tribes that did not have a central leader or formal government.

As the story goes, Saul was looking for one of his father's lost donkeys and sought help from the prophet Samuel (a seer). God had told Samuel that He would send him a man of Benjamin whom he should anoint king over God's people, and that man was Saul. Samuel secretly anointed Saul the first king of all the tribes of Israel before he was publicly selected by the people (10:17-24).

Saul was a competent military leader; however, a series of severe mistakes, beginning with an unauthorized sacrificial offering, started Saul's downfall. His downward spiral continued as he failed to eliminate all the Amalekites and their livestock as commanded by God. Then, disregarding a direct order from God, he decided to spare the life of King Agag along with some of the choice livestock. He tried to cover up his transgression by lying to Samuel and, in essence, lying to God. This disobedience was the last straw, as God would later withdraw His Spirit from Saul (16:14).

So, let's get back to David's story. Saul reigns as King over Israel, but God is not pleased with him because he refuses to follow God's instructions. He has made excuses, tried to blame others for his disobedience, and even built a monument to honor himself (15:10-12). Saul's continual rebellion and stubbornness caused God to reject him as King and to tell

Samuel, *"Fill your flask with olive oil and go to Bethlehem. Find a man named Jesse who lives there, for I have selected one of his sons to be my king."*

Samuel went to Bethlehem and prepared to anoint one of Jesse's sons as King of Israel. Jesse's first son Eliab was impressive, and Samuel thought this son would surely be the one God would have him anoint. However, God quickly reminded Samuel that *"people judge by outward appearance, but the Lord looks at the heart."*

All seven brothers stood before Samuel, but God did not choose any of them. Samuel then learned that another son was out tending his father's sheep, and the boy's name was David. God saw in David's young heart special qualities that greatly pleased Him.

> The Lord told Samuel, *"Arise, anoint him; for this is the one! So as David stood there among his brothers, Samuel took the flask of olive oil he had brought and anointed David with the oil. And the Spirit of the Lord came powerfully upon David from that day on."*

David was just a boy, probably between 10–15 years of age. Perhaps at this time, the Spirit of the Lord left Saul because he became troubled and couldn't sleep. One of Saul's servants mentioned that he knew of a shepherd boy who was skillful in playing the harp, and perhaps the soothing music would ease Saul's mind. David was summoned, and when Saul heard the gentle music of the harp, the distressing spirit left him, and he felt *refreshed and well*.

God was preparing David for his destiny by placing him in the king's court, where he could become acquainted with the business and general state of the kingdom. King Saul found favor with David, and when Saul did not need him, David went back and forth to tend his father's sheep at Bethlehem.

King Saul did not know God had secretly anointed David as the future king. But as Paul would later record:

"All things work together for good to those who love God, to those who are the called according to His purpose" (Romans 8:28).

During this time, the Philistines and Israelites gathered their armies for battle at Socoh in Judah. The Israeli army was on a mountain on one side, and the Philistine army was on the other side. The *Valley of Elah* lay between them.

The Philistines had a warrior and champion named **Goliath** who came from Gath. His height was *"six cubits and a span."* A cubit is the length from the elbow to the tip of the middle finger and is about 18 inches. The span is the distance from the thumb to the middle or little finger, when stretched apart to the full length, and is half a cubit (9 inches). Some ancient texts state that Goliath stood about 9 ½ to 11 feet tall. He had a bronze helmet on his head and was armed with a coat of mail that weighed five thousand shekels of bronze (78 pounds). He also had bronze armor on his legs and a javelin with an iron spearhead that is thought to weigh over 37 pounds. The spear's weight and all the armor could be well over 250 pounds.

This is where the story gets very interesting. Goliath challenged the Saul army to select a man to fight him. If the man can defeat Goliath, the Philistines will be servants of Saul. However, if Goliath defeated Saul's champion, then the Israelites would be servants of the Philistines. Goliath defied any man in the army of Israel to fight him.

When hearing the Philistine's words, Saul and all the Israelites were dismayed and terrified. This is precisely why Goliath issued the challenge. His coming out with full battle equipment and parading in front of the Israelite army was to strike fear into the Israelites' hearts. And Saul and his army had reason to be afraid because Goliath was a fearsome giant among men. King Saul was the leader of the Israel army, but the Spirit of the LORD had departed from him, and the regal qualities he once had were now given to David. The three oldest sons of Jesse; Eliab, Abinadab, and Shammah, had followed Saul to the battle.

One day Jesse told his son David, *"Take now for your brothers an ephah (*little over a bushel*) of this dried grain and these ten loaves and run to your brothers at the camp. And carry these ten cheeses to the captain of their thousand, and see how your brothers fare, and bring back news of them."* David rose early the next morning, left the sheep with a keeper, and went to the Israel army camp.

I can imagine what David saw as he came into the camp. Armies were gathered on each hillside, screaming and shouting at each other across the valley, and then the giant Goliath shouted his insults. Remember that Goliath never quit taunting and mocking the Israel army for forty mornings and evenings, especially King Saul. He called them all cowards. What a sight!

David delivered his supplies and greeted his brothers. He heard the roar of Goliath, and he saw the fear in the eyes of the Israel army. There was not one man among them who would fight Goliath. The situation had become so desperate that Saul offered a three-part bribe to the man who could fight and win against Goliath. This included a cash reward, his daughter's hand in marriage, and the champion would be exempt from certain taxes and obligations.

But these were not the rewards David was seeking. He was focused on the reputation of Israel and the honor of the living God (17:25-27). David asked the men standing near him, *"Who is this uncircumcised Philistine that he should defy the armies of the living God?"* He referred to Goliath as *"This uncircumcised Philistine."*

David's brothers, especially Eliab, were angry with David because they said that his pride and the insolence of his heart made him come to the camp to see the battle. He was an insignificant, worthless person with no right to speak with such bold words, and he had probably left the sheep in the wilderness unattended.

However, each of the men of the Israel army knew that David's words were correct. He wanted them to be courageous and protect the honor of Israel and God. David was most likely a teenager, probably 16-19 years old. David was not yet serving in the army, so he was under twenty years old (Numbers 1:3).

David showed more courage than anyone in the Israel army and told Saul he would fight Goliath. I am sure that Saul thought that the good news was that someone would finally fight Goliath, but the bad news was that it was a shepherd boy, and Goliath was a man of war from his youth. But David told Saul that while tending the sheep, he had killed a lion and a bear, and with God's help, he would do the same to Goliath. Throughout David's life, God was preparing him with faith to fight Goliath. And today would be that day.

Saul clothed David with armor, a helmet, a coat of mail, and a sword, but David told Saul that he could not walk with all that on his body. He removed all the armor, then chose five smooth stones from the brook and placed one in his sling. As David drew near the Philistine, he trusted the Lord. With his shield-bearer in front of him, Goliath kept coming closer to David and said, *"Am I a dog, that you come at me with sticks?"* And the Philistine cursed David and his God. *"Come here,"* he said, *"and I'll give your flesh to the birds and the wild animals!"*

David replied, *"You come against me with sword and spear and javelin, but I come against you in the name of the Lord Almighty, the God of the armies of Israel, whom you have defied. This day the Lord will deliver you into my hands, and I'll strike you down and cut off your head. This very day I will give the carcasses of the Philistine army to the birds and the wild animals, and the whole world will know that there is a God in Israel. All those gathered here will know that it is not by sword or spear that the Lord saves; for the battle is the Lord's, and he will give all of you into our hands."*

If it hadn't been established before, it is certainly settled now. This is not a fair fight. It isn't Goliath and his armor-bearer against David. It is Goliath and his armor-bearer against David and the Lord God of Israel. David was bold, but bold in God, not in himself. He knew the battle belonged to the LORD.

David took a stone from his pouch, sprinted toward Goliath, and slung the stone, striking the Philistine. The stone sank into Goliath's forehead, and he fell face down on the ground. David fought on behalf of all Israel, and if the Israel army wasn't trusting in the Lord, David would trust in the Lord for them.

The Israeli army thought, "Goliath is so big, we can't beat him," but David thought, "Goliath is so big, I can't miss him."

David stood over the Philistine, took the giant's sword, and cut off Goliath's head. When the Philistines saw that their hero was dead, they turned and ran. They had agreed to surrender to Israel if their champion lost, but they did not. The soldiers of Israel pursued and defeated the Philistines. David brought Goliath's head to Jerusalem, and he placed the Philistine's weapons in his tent. The king embraced David as his own, and from that day forward, David lived in the king's palace.

Saul's son, Jonathan, and David became extremely good friends, but the real trouble was just beginning. When the men returned home after David had killed the Philistine, women came out from all the towns of Israel to meet King Saul by singing and dancing. As they danced, they sang,  *"Saul has slain his thousands, and David his tens of thousands."* This made Saul angry, thinking David was trying to take away his kingdom. From this point on, Saul became very dangerous. He later gave

David command over a thousand men and sent him into battles where he hoped David would be killed. But David was successful in all his campaigns. Saul saw how successful he was and hated David even more.

Saul offered his older daughter, Merab, to David in marriage, but when the time came, she was given in marriage to Adriel of Meholah. Saul's daughter **Michal** was in love with David, and when they told Saul about it, he was pleased. But he was pleased because he thought she might be a snare to him, which would help the Philistines.

David was concerned that since he was only a poor man and little known, it was no small matter to become the king's son-in-law. Saul responded that he wanted no other price for the bride than a hundred Philistine foreskins to take revenge on his enemies. Saul hoped that the Philistines would kill David. David and his men went out and killed two hundred Philistines and brought back their foreskins. Saul gave his daughter Michal in marriage, but Saul's anger increased against David for the rest of his days.

Saul even spoke of David's death to his son Jonathan and all the attendants. On one occasion, the evil spirit from the Lord came upon Saul as he was sitting in his house with a spear in his hand. Saul tried to hit him with the javelin as David played the lyre, but missed. This evil spirit was likely part of God's judgment upon Saul for his disobedience. David achieved increasing success in battle, and his name became well-known.

On another occasion, Saul was irate and sent men to David's house to watch it and then kill him in the morning. But David's wife Michal took an idol (teraphim—possibly a life-size figure or bust) and laid it on the bed. She then covered it with a garment and put some goats' hair on the head, possibly to imitate the effect of a man's hair around the head. When Saul's men approached, Michael told them David was ill and in bed. But when the men entered, David had fled through a window and escaped.

David asked his good friend Jonathan what great sin he had committed that made Saul so angry with him. Jonathan didn't know but tried to comfort him. David was scheduled to attend the monthly new moon meeting with the king, but he did not go. Saul asked Jonathan where David was, and when Jonathan said he had some business to take care of with his family, Saul became very angry and threw his javelin at his son Jonathan. He said that if David were alive, his kingdom would be threatened. Jonathan was shamed and saddened, and if David stayed there, he would undoubtedly be killed.

Jonathan told David what had happened, and they embraced and cried heavily, knowing that this could be the last time they would ever see each other again. However, they made a covenant between each other and their seed to follow that they would always be good friends.

David flees the area and meets a priest in *Nob* named  **Ahimelech**. He tells the priest a false story about being on a secret mission for Saul to obtain his assistance. David states that his mission was so urgent that he did not bring any weapon, and the priest states, "*The sword of Goliath the Philistine, whom you killed in the Valley of Elah, is here; it is wrapped in a cloth behind the ephod. If you want it, take it; there is no sword here but that one.*" And David took the sword.

David later went to the *cave of Adullam,* where he met his family and other friends. About four hundred men were with David, and he became their commander. David then met with the *king of Moab* and asked that the king allow his father and mother to stay with him until God shows David what to do.

Saul heard that David met with the priest Ahimelech at Nob, and that he had been given provisions and the sword of Goliath the Philistine. Saul summoned the priest and all the men of his family and asked why they were conspiring against him. Ahimelech answered the king by saying that none of Saul's servants were as loyal as David, and that he should be highly respected in Saul's household. Saul then ordered the guards to kill all of them because they had sided with David. The king's officials were unwilling to raise a hand to strike the priests of the Lord, but *Doeg the Edomite* turned and struck all the people down.

David knew Saul was again plotting against him and asked Abiathar, the priest, to bring him the ephod. The high priests wore this ephod (starting with Aaron, as mentioned in Exodus 28:4). The breastplate of the ephod contained the Urim and Thummim, gemstones used to inquire of God to determine His will in any given situation.

David asked the Lord if Saul planned to come to Keilah and destroy the town because of him, and the answer was "yes." David then asked if the citizens of Keilah would surrender David to Saul, and again, the answer was "yes." David and his six hundred men left Keilah and stayed in the wilderness strongholds and hills of the Desert of Ziph. Day after day, Saul searched for him, but God did not give David into his hands.

The Ziphites approached Saul at Gibeah and said they would help find and capture David. At this time, David and his men were in the Desert of Maon, in the Arabah south of Jeshimon, and once Saul was told this, he went in pursuit. David and Saul were on opposite sides of the mountain, but Saul and his forces were closing quickly. A messenger suddenly came to Saul, saying that the Philistines were raiding the land. Saul broke off his pursuit of David and went to meet the Philistines. This place is called *Sela Hammahlekoth*. David went up from there and lived in the strongholds of *En Gedi*.

But Saul was not one to give up. After he returned from pursuing the Philistines, he took three thousand able young men and set out to look for David and his men near the *Crags of the Wild Goats*. On his way, he came across a cave and went  in to relieve himself. Little did he know that David and his men were far back in the cave. The men were happy that they would finally be able to kill Saul. But David crept up unnoticed and cut off a corner of Saul's robe.

Afterwards, David told his men, *"The Lord forbid that I should do such a thing to my master, the Lord's anointed, or lay my hand on him; for he is the anointed of the Lord."* The men did not attack, and Saul left the cave.

David came out of the cave and asked the king why he would listen to anyone who said David would harm him when just that day in the cave, he could have killed him. David then showed him the piece of the robe he had cut off earlier. Saul wept, said he had mistreated David, and returned home.

The prophet Samuel died at around 90, and all Israel assembled and mourned for him. They buried him at his home in *Ramah*. David then moved down into the *Desert of Paran* (Faran). This is one of the places where the Israelites spent part of their 40 years of wandering after the Exodus. It was also home to *Ishmael* and a place of refuge for David.

We are now told of a man named **Nabal** who was very wealthy and had a thousand goats and three thousand sheep on his property at *Carmel (a city of Judah)*. But he was mean in his dealings. David had heard it was shearing time for the sheep and sent ten young men to greet Nabal in his name. David had been watching over the fellow's property in the wilderness so that nothing went missing. David was asking for any provisions that Nabal could provide them.

The young men gave the message to Nabal, and he said that he didn't know this "David" and why should he give his bread, water, and meat to unknown strangers. When this response was given to David, he immediately told the men to strap on their swords. David's servants told Nabal's beautiful wife **Abigail** the insults Nabal had given them, and that David was insulted and heading this way. She quickly loaded two hundred loaves of bread, two skins of wine, five dressed sheep, five seahs (a dry measure equal to about 9 quarts) of roasted grain, a hundred cakes of raisins, and two hundred cakes of pressed figs and loaded them on donkeys.

She met David and his men and quickly got off her donkey, bowed before David, and apologized for Nabal's actions. She then presented David with all the provisions for the donkeys.

David was pleased that no blood would be shed and thanked her. About ten days later, the Lord struck Nabal, and he died. When David heard that Nabal was dead, he sent word to Abigail, asking her to become his wife, and she accepted. David had also married *Ahinoam of Jezreel*, and they both were his wives (25:44). But Saul had given his daughter Michal, David's wife, to Paltiel, son of Laish, who was from Gallim.

David is now in the *wilderness of Ziph* and is once again on the run from King Saul. David finds Saul's camp, and the entire army is asleep; a situation orchestrated by the Lord. David and his companion, **Abishai**, creep into the camp, and they find Saul and **Abner**, *the son of Ner, the commander of the army*. Abishai urges David to kill Saul, but David refuses to harm the Lord's anointed king. Instead, David takes Saul's spear and water jug as evidence that he was there and could have killed the king.

David stood on top of the hill some distance away and called out to Abner and chastised him for being a poor guardian of the king. David tells him to look for the spear and water jug near the king's head. Saul recognizes David's voice, and once again, David asks Saul why he is pursuing him. David returned Saul's spear, and Saul said, "*May you be blessed, David my son; you will do great things and surely triumph.*"

David went on his way, and Saul returned home. But David thought to himself, "*One of these days I will be destroyed by the hand of Saul. The best thing I can do is to escape to the land of the Philistines. Then Saul will give up searching for me anywhere in Israel, and I will slip out of his hand.*"

Saul seems to love David one moment and hate him the next. David takes his 600 men and his two wives, Ahinoam and Abigail, and goes to *Gath, a country of the Philistines*. When Saul was told that David had fled to Gath, he no longer searched for him.

Achish, the king of Gath, likes David and grants him the city of *Ziklag*, where David lived for one year and four months. During this time, he engages in military activities and raids against the old inhabitants of the land, including the Gershurites, Gezrites, and Amalekites—lands originally meant to be conquered by Joshua. These were all *"Bedaween"* tribes, the scourge of the Israelitish families dwelling south of Canaan. David is a brutal warrior and kills both men and women and seizes their livestock. David keeps the details of his actions hidden from Achish, who believes that David is loyal to him and will remain with him forever.

Once again, the Philistines gathered their armies together for battle against Israel. But the Philistine army was so large this time that King Saul became extremely afraid. He was so afraid that he sought guidance from the Lord, but God had moved away from him. In desperation, Saul sought information from the spirits. Saul had previously expelled all the spiritists and mediums from the land, but obviously, some remained.

Disguising himself, he met a **witch in Endor** and asked her to bring up Samuel the prophet, which she did. Samuel wanted to know why he was awakened, and Saul told Samuel of the Philistine problem. Samuel responded, *"if God isn't talking to you, what makes you think I will?"* Samuel further reminds Saul that God stopped dealing with him because he didn't obey God's instructions.

Samuel then says, *"Further God has already given your kingdom to David, and by the way; this time tomorrow you and your sons will be dead after a battle with the Philistines."* The woman was shocked and bewildered, and Saul was lifeless.

So, was the apparition the witch of Endor saw Samuel himself? It was not an illusion she produced because she screamed in surprise when she saw Samuel. The text does not say that the spirit "appeared to be Samuel; " it directly refers to the spirit as "Samuel." And the spirit spoke the truth; the message Saul received was accurate. Perhaps in this case, God allowed Samuel to return and give King Saul the news of his coming defeat and death.

The Philistines are set to battle against Israel, but the king of Gath was told by his men not to allow David to fight. They were angry and afraid that David might have a change of heart and decide to support Saul and Israel. Everyone knows of David's reputation as a warrior, so Achish told David he couldn't fight with him, and David and his men went in peace back to Ziklag.

Once David and his men got to Ziklag, they saw that the town had been raided, set on fire, and looted by the Amalekites. They had also taken David's two wives and the wives and children of his men. There was much anger and grieving, but David went to God for support. God encouraged David to pursue the kidnappers and retrieve all they had lost.

Four hundred of David's men went with him, but two hundred stayed back because they were too distraught to fight. While pursuing the kidnappers, they came across an Egyptian slave who was part of the Amalekites' invasion at Ziklag. The man was ill and probably left to die. David fed the Egyptian and was given information on where the Amalekites went to loot next. David and his men found the Amalekites, battled, and recovered everything taken. They even took all the Amalekites' flocks and herds, saying, *"This is David's plunder"* as they left.

Hard feelings developed between the men who pursued the Amalekites and those who stayed behind, but David was a wise leader and stated that the Lord had preserved and delivered them all. They would all share in the plunder. David even sent some of the plunder to the elders of Judah, who were his friends, saying, *"Here is a gift for you from the plunder of the Lord's enemies."*

The Philistines fought against Israel, and many Israelites fell dead on *Mount Gilboa*. Saul's sons **Jonathan, Abinadab, and Malki-Shua** were killed, and archers overtook Saul, critically wounding him. Saul asked his armor-bearer to, *"Draw your sword and run me through, or these uncircumcised fellows will come and run me through and abuse me."* But his armor-bearer was terrified and would not do it, so Saul took his sword and fell on it. When the armor-bearer saw that Saul was dead, he fell on his sword and died with him.

Saul and his three sons and his armor-bearer and all his men died together that same day. Later, when the Philistines came to strip the dead, they cut off Saul's head, stripped off his armor, and sent messengers throughout the land of the Philistines to proclaim the news. Saul's armor was placed in the *Temple of Ashtoreth*, and they fastened Saul and his sons' bodies to the wall of *Beth Shan*.

Once the people of *Jabesh Gilead* heard what the Philistines had done to Saul, a few valiant men marched through the night to Beth Shan, took down the bodies of Saul and his sons from the wall, and went to Jabesh, where they burned them. The bones were then buried under a tamarisk tree at Jabesh.

Three days later, a man from Saul's camp told David the bad news about Saul and his sons. David asked the man how he knew this information was accurate, and the man wanted to act as the hero, so he told David that he was Saul's actual armor bearer and took credit for putting Saul out of his misery after being wounded. He thought David would give him a position in his army, but David asked the man why he wasn't respectful enough to honor Saul, the Lord's anointed. David had the man killed.

David was saddened by Saul and Jonathan's deaths and wrote a song with the famous quote, "How are the mighty fallen?" In the song, he expressed his love for his brother Jonathan.

The Lord had David go to the city of *Hebron*, and *here the men anointed David as their captain and the official king over Judah.* While this was happening, *Abner*, Saul's surviving military captain, made **Ishbosheth,** a son of Saul, the king over the other 11 tribes of Israel. Ishbosheth was 40 but would only govern for two years over the tribes. David was the king in Hebron for seven and a half years.

Abner and his men instigated a fight between some of *Joab and David's servants,* and they let the young men fight to see who the strongest warriors were. Unfortunately, all twenty died as they killed each other fighting to the death. Joab and his men were furious and chased Abner and his men. Abner, a trained killer, warned *Joab's brother Asahel,* who was very fast, to stop the pursuit so he wouldn't have to kill him. Unfortunately, Abner wound up killing Asahel, creating a *bitter rivalry between Joab and Abner.*

Saul's remaining son, Ishbosheth, who took over the kingdom, had a falling out with *Abner*, the chief guard of Saul, over a concubine of Saul's, and Abner resigned. He began a campaign to join Israel under the house of Judah and David. Before this could happen, David told Abner that Michal, his first wife and Saul's daughter, would have to be returned to him. And she was.

To celebrate Abner joining the team, David makes him a feast, but *Joab, David's chief guard*, isn't there during the acceptance of Abner. When he heard of the alliance between David and Abner, he was very upset and told David that Abner was just there to spy. Joab then killed Abner to avenge his brother, and once David was told, he put the blood on Joab and his house forever. David gave Abner a proper burial and said that Israel had lost a great man in the death of Abner.

Baanah and Rechab were captains of units commanded by **Ish** (Ishbosheth). After Abner was killed, they were concerned for their lives and thought David would destroy the house of Saul. To show their allegiance to David, the incoming king, and secure jobs in his administration, they decided to kill Ish and bring his head to David. This was done, but David respected Saul's house and was angry with the two men. He commanded his men to kill them both immediately and to cut off their hands and feet and hang them over a pool in *Hebron*. Killing them in such a terrible fashion would show David's disapproval of Ish's assassination and of any further attempts on the house of Saul. Ish was buried properly near *Abner.*

David had become a very effective leader, and all the tribes of Israel wanted him as king. David and his army marched to Jerusalem to attack the Jebusites, and David captured the *fortress of Zion.* David then took up residence in the fortress and called it the **City of David**. He became more and more powerful because the Lord God Almighty was with him. *Hiram, king of Tyre,* sent envoys to David, along with cedar logs, carpenters, and stonemasons, and they built a palace for David.

When the Philistines heard that David had been anointed king over Israel, they went up in full force to search for him. But David heard about it, and with God's support, he went to *Baal Perazim* and defeated them.

Later, the Philistines intended to do battle in the *Valley of Rephaim.* David inquired of the Lord, who answered, *"Do not go straight up, but circle around behind them and attack them in front of the poplar trees. As soon as you hear the sound of marching in the tops of the poplar trees, move quickly, because that will mean the Lord has gone out in front of you to strike the Philistine army."* David did as the Lord commanded him, and he struck down the Philistines from Gibeon to Gezer.

David began to marry more concubines and had more sons and daughters. He was thirty years old when he began to reign, and his rulership lasted forty years. The Philistines still waged war, and before each battle, David would speak to God and ask if he should engage in combat and if he would win. David always won.

David and a chosen group of 30,000 men traveled to *Gibeah*  to retrieve the **Ark of God** (*Ark of the Covenant*) and take it back to Israel. They were all joyful that the Ark of the Covenant would be removed from the *House of Abinadab* in Gibeah and taken to its home in Israel. The Lord's presence would be back with His people. As the ark was being transported, the oxen pulled the cart stumbled, and a man named **Uzzah** (u-zaw) took hold of the ark. God's anger burned against Uzzah, and He struck him dead.

Uzzah's punishment appears extreme for what we might consider a good deed. However, there are several reasons why God took such severe action:

(1) God had given Moses and Aaron specific instructions about the Tent of Meeting and the movement of the Ark of the Covenant.

> *"After Aaron and his sons have finished covering the holy furnishings and all the holy articles, and when the camp is ready to move, the Kohathites are to come to do the carrying. But they must not touch the holy things or they will die. The Kohathites are to carry those things that are in the Tent of Meeting"* (Numbers 4:15).

No matter how innocently it was done, touching the ark was in direct violation of God's law and was to result in death.

(2) David took men with him to collect the ark, rather than allowing the Levites to bring it to him. That was a great mistake, since it ought never to have been put upon a cart, old or new. It was to be borne upon men's shoulders, and carried by Levites only, and those of the family of Kohath, using the poles prescribed (Exodus 25:12-14; Numbers 7:9). Not following God's precise instructions would be seen as not revering God's words when He spoke to them and an act of disobedience.

(3) The Ark stayed at Abinadab's house, where his sons, Uzzah and Ahio, may have become accustomed to its presence. Uzzah, having been around the Ark in his own home, could very likely forget the holiness that it represented.

(4) It says that the oxen stumbled, but the cart didn't fall, and neither did the Ark. Perhaps Uzzah, for a second, felt that he had to act. The result for Uzzah was tragic. David was stunned and unsure how to bring the Ark of the Covenant back to his city, and for the time, they decided to leave the Ark of the Covenant at *Obededom's* home. The Ark of the Covenant stayed there for three months, and while it remained there, God began to bless Obededom's house. This made David and his men even more determined to return the Ark of the Covenant to Israel. The book of Chronicles explains how they correctly brought the Ark of the Covenant back to Israel. Everyone in Israel celebrated the return of the Ark of the Covenant except David's first wife, Michal. David was leaping and dancing like a common man, and she wanted him to behave like a "King." But David told her he was rejoicing before God, the same God who chose him even above her father Saul to be ruler over all Israel. David said he would play music and dance before the God of Israel, and everyone would honor him.

David thought of building God a magnificent temple and shared his thoughts with Nathan, the prophet. Nathan recommended that David do what was in his heart. However, God said "No" to David's offer because David was a man of war, and God wanted a man of peace to build His temple (1 Chr. 22:8-10). God promised that He would make the House of David, an enduring legacy for David long after his death.

In Luke 1:31-33 we read, *"For unto us a Child is born, unto us a Son is given; and the government will be upon His shoulder.... Upon the throne of David and over His kingdom, to order it and establish it...from that time forward, even forever."*

God's promise of a house for David is completely fulfilled in Jesus Christ, who will reign on David's throne forever. David was a legendary warrior, and those he defeated and kept alive served him as tributaries (subordinates) and servants. He defeated Hadadezer, *the king of Zobah*, and took 1,700 horsemen and chariots, 20,000 soldiers, and reestablished Israel's border at the river Euphrates. The *Syrians* tried to aid the king of Zobah, but David destroyed 22,000 of them for meddling in his business affairs.

David made his enemies his servants, and many began to send him gifts to stay in good grace with him. David dedicated all the gifts he received to the Lord and kept them as a national treasure. God was with him, and David was famous for his war exploits and defeating great kings and nations.

 There is mention of David's sons being priests. A priest is a mediator between God and man. How could they have been, when only Levite descendants of Aaron were supposed to be priests? Some have suggested that the Hebrew word *kōhēn*, the general word for priest through the Old Testament, may have another or a broader meaning, such as *"royal advisors"* or *"chief officials."*

Maybe they were considered priests in *the order of* **Melchizedek**, *(mal-chez-da-dek)* an old Canaanite name meaning *"My King Is Righteousness."* The Bible uses the phrase *"the order of"* to point to a lineage. David's sons could have had the inherited title and performed whatever duties were associated with the office. Still, these duties would not have included any of the functions reserved for the Levitical priests (Hebrews 7:1).

Melchizedek is described as the king of Salem, which would later become Jerusalem, and a priest of God Most High. Abram recognized Melchizedek's priesthood by tithing the possessions he had taken in battle. Jesus' future role is described as the Great High Priest, using Melchizedek's role to illustrate Jesus' priesthood and kingship. Jesus provides an eternal priesthood to save us from our sins for eternity, *"not based on a regulation as to his ancestry but on the basis of the power of an indestructible life."* Jesus is still our eternal High Priest.

Even though David was a great warrior, he was also a very compassionate person. He asked if any of Saul's house was left so that he could show courtesy to their house for Jonathan's sake. David was told that Mephibosheth, one of Jonathan's sons, had survived, and David immediately sent for him. Saul's servant Ziba was appointed to take care of Mephibosheth.

The father of the *Ammonite king Hanun* died, and King David sent a delegation to convey his condolences. The Ammonite king misinterpreted the gesture, thinking David's men were spies. He humiliated them and sent them back to

Israel. Later, realizing their mistake, the Ammonites prepared for war and hired Aramean forces (mercenaries). David led Israel's army to a decisive victory, and peace returned when the Arameans accepted Israel's dominance.

One evening while in Jerusalem, David walked around on his palace's roof and saw a beautiful woman bathing. The woman was **Bathsheba**, the daughter of Eliam and the wife of **Uriah** the Hittite. David, the king, sent for her, and they slept together. The woman conceived and told David that she was pregnant. The king's reaction was an attempt to hide his sin. David sent for his soldier Uriah the Hittite with the intention that Uriah would go home and sleep with his wife. But Uriah slept at the entrance to the palace with all his master's servants and did not go down to his house.

Uriah told David, "*The ark and Israel and Judah are staying in tents, and my commander Joab and my lord's men are camped in the open country. How could I go to my house to eat and drink and make love to my wife? As surely as you live, I will not do such a thing!*"

David then wrote a letter to Joab and sent it with Uriah. The note said, "*Put Uriah out in front where the fighting is fiercest. Then withdraw from him so he will be struck down and die.*" The next day, Uriah was placed at the front of the battle and was killed, and Joab then sent David a complete account of the battle.

The messenger told David, "*The men overpowered us and came out against us in the open, but we drove them back to the entrance of the city gate. Then the archers shot arrows at your servants from the wall, and some of the king's men died. Moreover, your servant Uriah the Hittite is dead.*"

David told the messenger, "*Say this to Joab: 'Don't let this upset you; the sword devours one as well as another. Press the attack against the city and destroy it.' Say this to encourage Joab.*"

When Uriah's wife heard that her husband was dead, she mourned for him, and after the time of mourning was over,

David brought her to his house, and she became his wife. But David had displeased the Lord.

God sent *the prophet Nathan* to see David. Nathan begins with a parable about a rich man with many sheep and a poor man with just one sheep, whom he treats like his daughter. When a traveler visited the rich man, he used the poor man's only sheep instead of one of his many sheep. The story made David furious, and he said that whoever did this deserved to die and should also have to restore the poor man fourfold because of his actions. David was angry that the rich man had no shame or pity. Nathan then revealed that David was the man.

God reminded David that He had made him king over Israel and delivered him from all his enemies. David took responsibility and confessed, "*I have sinned against the LORD.*" David was guilty of adultery, and judgment was placed upon his house in the form of ongoing violence. David repented, but the child conceived with Bathsheba died a week later. David's attendants were afraid to tell him that the child was dead because they thought he might do something desperate.

David noticed that his attendants were whispering among themselves, and he realized the child was dead. He got up from the ground, washed, changed his clothes, and went into the house of the Lord and worshipped. He then went to his own home and ate.

His attendants questioned him and said, "*While the child was alive, you fasted and wept, but now that the child is dead, you get up and eat!*" David answered, "*While the child was still alive, I fasted and wept. I thought, 'Who knows? The Lord may be gracious to me and let the child live.' But now that he is dead, why should I go on fasting? Can I bring him back again? <u>I will go to him, but he will not return to me.</u>*"

David's household experienced further hardship in later years. In total, four of David's sons suffered untimely deaths. Our actions always have consequences, even for great men like David, who God loves and protects.

Bathsheba and David had another child named **Solomon,** and God loved the child. God even had Nathan tell David that the LORD called the child *Jedidiah*—Hebrew for *"Beloved of the Lord."* The names Jedidiah and David are related in that the name David means *"beloved."*

David had a very handsome son named **Absalom** and a sister called **Tamar**. **Amnon**, another son of David (a different mother than Absalom and Tamar), was in love with Absalom's sister Tamar. Amnon pretended to be physically sick and persuaded King David to send Tamar to visit him. Amnon had the room emptied of officials so that only Tamar remained, and he ultimately raped her.

After this, he told her to get out and that he hated her. Tamar told her brother Absalom what happened, which was reported to King David with little result. Absalom acted like it wasn't a big deal, yet he planned revenge on Amnon. Two years later, when all the king's sons were attending a party, Absalom commanded his servants to kill Amnon, and it was done. Absalom fled to Geshur, where his mother and Tamar, his sister, were from, and he stayed there for three years.

Joab, David's captain, thinks that David's mind is set more on Absalom, his son, than on his kingly duties, so he tried to get the king out of his rut by sending a woman to speak with him about a situation like his own. She told a story about her two sons who'd gotten into a fight, and one killed the other. The family demanded that the other son be killed, and she was distraught because now she would lose both sons and her husband, who was also dead. The name of the family would not be carried on. David promised her that nothing would happen to her remaining son.

Before leaving, she asked the king why he judged one way with her, but another for himself. She brought up the Absalom and Amnon situation. Why did the king not require his son Absalom to return home from his banished state? David realized he had been tricked by Joab and instructed that

Absalom be brought back to Judah—and maybe that was a mistake.

Absalom was cagey and prepared a subtle power move to take over David's kingdom. He positioned a small team of his followers near the gate of the entryway to the king's court. Absalom would then intercept anyone coming to the king for a judgment about any issue and handle the matter in a kind and loving way. Slowly, he stole the hearts of the people.

Towards the end of David's reign, Absalom asked David if he could go to Hebron and pay a vow he had made while he was banished in Geshur of Syria. The king permitted this, but Absalom had spies blow a trumpet throughout Israel shouting, "*Absalom rules in Hebron!*" As time passed, the nation was strongly behind Absalom, and David's people finally realized what was happening. Instead of going to war with his son, David left and lived in the wilderness. David sent *Hushai* back and forth to Jerusalem to work as a spy in Absalom's cabinet.

A man named **Ziba**, *the servant of Mephibosheth*, met with David and provided items he could use during his stay in the wilderness. Mephibosheth, the son of Jonathan, was patiently waiting for the house of Israel to be restored to him and his father, Saul's house.

David's *chief counselor, Hushai,* works as a double agent. During one of their daily meetings, Absalom asked both of his counselors, **Ahithophel** and Hushai, what he should do. It was suggested that Absalom sleep with his father's concubines, who were left behind. This lewd act would show the people that he was truly finished with his father, David. Absalom did what was suggested.

Absalom then sought counsel from his administration to hunt his father, David, and kill him. *Ahithophel* suggests that they send 12,000 men to hunt and then kill David. *Hushai* disagreed with Ahithophel's counsel and reminded Absalom that David was a man of war. He had hidden and evaded Saul; even if they find David, he will be hard to defeat. Hushai reminded the group that David still had mighty men of war around him, suggesting they first find David, circle the area slowly, and then capture him.

Hushai, still working for David, told both Zadok and Abiathar, David's priests, about this plan. Hushai also warned them to tell the king to move from the base he was at in the wilderness so he would not be trapped. David and all his men crossed over the Jordan. Meanwhile, back in Jerusalem, Ahithophel saw that his counsel wasn't taken and figured it was the end of his career. He then put his house in order and killed himself.

At this point, David divides his army into thirds, appointing Joab, Abishai, and Ittai the Gittite over each part. They prepare to fight Absalom and his army. Even though David states that he'll also go out and fight, the people object, saying he's much too important. David stays behind but tells his commanders not to kill Absalom and to deal gently with him if they find him.

The battle takes place in the *forest of Ephraim*. David's troops slaughter Absalom's men, with casualties running up to twenty thousand. During the fight, Absalom is riding on his mule when his long hair gets caught in a tree branch, and he is lifted off the mule, stuck in midair. The soldiers are mindful of what David said about not killing Absalom; however, Joab comes along, grabs three spears, and sticks them all at once into Absalom's heart, killing him. The battle ends, and they bury Absalom in a pit in the woods, covering it with stones. David is then told that Absalom is dead.

The Absalom rebellion ends, but a man named **Sheba** gets all the people of Israel (except Judah) to follow him in rebellion. To deal with Sheba's rebellion, David sends **Amasa** to summon the people of Judah, but he takes too long, so David tells *Abishai* to take his men and pursue Sheba. Joab brings his men along with Abishai, and when they meet up with Amasa, Joab (likely remembering how Amasa replaced him) takes out his sword and slices open Amasa's stomach.

Sheba is trapped in a city called *Abel, in Beth-Maacah*. As David's men prepare to besiege the city, a wise woman tells Joab that this is a peaceful city and that they don't want any trouble. Joab says he's not looking for trouble, he just wants to capture Sheba and kill him. The people of Abel then agree to kill Sheba, and they chop his head off and throw it over the city walls to Joab. The troops head back to Jerusalem, and with Amasa dead, Joab is again the General in charge of the whole army.

A famine takes place in Israel and lasts for more than three years. David asks the Lord why the famine is taking place in his kingdom, and the answer is that Saul broke a vow and killed the Gibeonites, and the matter needs to be corrected. To fix the issue with the Gibeonites, the house of Saul needs to pay dearly. David asked the Gibeonites how he could correct the broken vow, and they demanded that seven of Saul's sons be killed as an atonement. David had no choice but to do as they asked, except for Jonathan's son, Mephibosheth. It was tragic but necessary to stop the famine. David then retrieved the bones of Saul and Jonathan and buried them in the country of Benjamin with Saul's father Kish.

Once again, the Philistines go to war against Israel, and during the battle, David grew faint and was nearly killed by the sons of the giants. This is when Israel decided that David was too valuable and should no longer come out to battle.

Many other battles between Israel and the Philistines occurred, and in one at *Gob, Elhanan son of Jair the Bethlehemite* killed the brother of Goliath the Gittite, who had a spear with a shaft like a weaver's rod. In still another battle, which took place at Gath, there was a huge man with six fingers on each hand and six toes on each foot—twenty-four in all. When he taunted Israel, **Jonathan, son of Shimeah**, David's brother, killed him.

David praises God as his rock, fortress, deliverer, shield, horn of his salvation, and stronghold. He speaks of God's deliverance, pulling him out of deep waters, symbolizing grave danger or death, and bringing him into a spacious place of safety because of God's delight in him. David attributes his rescue to his righteousness and faithfulness to God's laws. David concludes his song with high praises to God, expressing trust in His promises and celebrating the victories God has given him over his enemies.

We now come to what is thought to be David's last speech to the people of Israel. He told them that God's word was in his mouth and that whoever rules over men must be just and fear God. David told the people that God made an everlasting covenant with him and the house of Judah. He then acknowledged the valiant men who had been with him since the days he was running from Saul.

A story was told of a time David thirsted, and these mighty men went out of a cave surrounded by Philistines and brought back water for David to drink. But David humbly chose not to drink it because the men had put their lives at risk for him. So out of respect, he poured it on the ground to the Lord.

We end the Book of Samuel by describing what David had done to anger God. David decided to number the children of Israel by taking a census, which was not supposed to be done (Numbers 1:49). Even though Joab was against it, the king's word prevailed. It took them nearly ten months, and they discovered Judah had 500,000 men. Shortly after, David realized he'd made a terrible mistake in doing this census and confessed before God. The reason why David numbered the people is not explicitly told in scripture, but it is implied that David did not trust God and was worried about the nation's military power (1 Chronicles 21:3-4). Perhaps he wanted glory in the number of people available to him as king and wanted to see his strength.

To remedy this issue, **Gad**, *David's seer*, came and said God offers David three consequences. He could have:

1. seven years of famine in the land,

2. three months of running from his enemies, *or*

3. three days of pestilence in the land.

David chose to have the three days of pestilence from the Lord. David hoped God would have mercy, and He did—He only destroyed seventy thousand men. God even allowed David to see the angel with the sword stretched out in his hand over the city of Jerusalem. When David saw the destruction, he petitioned God to destroy his house and not the innocent people of the land who had nothing to do with his decision to number the people.

Gad told David to build an altar and offer sacrifices to the Lord to stop the plague entirely. David bought land and an altar from a man named **Araunah**. The man wanted to give the land and the altar to David for free, but David refused to receive anything for free to offer to God. David offered a sacrifice to God on the altar, and the plague was stopped.

King David reigned over Israel for 40 years and died in 837 BC at age 70. His death was peaceful and natural. David "*died at a good old age, having enjoyed long life, wealth and honor*" (1 Chronicles 29:28). He united all the tribes of Israel under a single monarch and is an essential figure in Judaism, Christianity, and Islam. He is known for his bravery, piety, and leadership, and is considered one of Israel's greatest kings.

Additional Information:

According to the Bible, King David had many wives, although only eight were named. (1) David's first wife was **Michal**, the daughter of King Saul. (2) David's second wife was **Abigail**. She was originally the wife of Nabal, an evil man who disrespected David. (3) David's next wife, Bathsheba, was originally the wife of Uriah the Hittite. The other five named wives of David were **Ahinoam, Maacah, Haggith, Abital**, and **Eglah** (2 Samuel 3:25; 1 Chronicles 3:13). According to 2 Samuel 5:13, David married more wives in Jerusalem, but how many is unknown. He also had an unknown number of concubines.

David had at least twenty-one children by his wives, plus an unknown number by his many concubines. These are the named children and the mother: Amnon *(Ahinoam)*, **Daniel** *(Abigail)*, **Absalom** (*Maakah*), **Adonijah** (*Haggith*), **Shephatiah** *(Abital)*, **Ithream** (*Eglah*), **Shimea** *(Bathsheba)*, **Shobab** *(Bathsheba)*, **Nathan** *(Bathsheba),* and **Solomon** *(Bathsheba).* (Solomon was the author of most of the Proverbs, the Song of Solomon, and the book of Ecclesiastes).

David's remaining children were born in Jerusalem, but little is known about them: **Ibhar**, **Elishama**, **Eliphelet**, **Nogah**, **Nepheg**, **Japhia**, *another* **Elishama**, **Eliada**, *another* **Eliphelet**, and **Tamar**.

David had a son named **Jerimoth**, mentioned in 2 Chronicles 11:18, but it's unclear if this is one of the sons mentioned above, using another name, or if he was one of David's sons by a concubine. David likely had many more sons and daughters than recorded in Scripture, as he had more wives and concubines than shown (1 Chronicles 3:9).

David is a main character in the Old Testament and is mentioned in several other books such as 1st and 2nd Samuel, 1st Kings, and 1st Chronicles. Nearly half of the Psalms are attributed to him. Sixty-six chapters are written about David in the Old Testament, and fifty references to him are made in the New Testament.

The books of Chronicles, Samuel, and Kings are "**the synoptical gospels.**" These three parallel each other and cover the same general incidents, often from a different point of view—the books center around God's love for David.

King Solomon and the Temples

Before we look into Solomon's life, it would be beneficial to remind the new reader that Solomon's renowned biblical father was King David. David was born in Bethlehem to a family of the Hebrew tribe of Judah. As a child, he tended to sheep and developed skills in music and combat. David had much interaction (good and bad) with Saul, the reigning king of

Israel, and David became a national hero by slaying the Philistine giant, Goliath. After King Saul's death, David was anointed as the new king of Israel and united all the tribes of Israel under a single monarch and established Jerusalem as the capital.

David wanted to build a house for the God of Israel, but the Lord told him:

"You have shed much blood and have waged great wars. You shall not build a house to my name, because you have shed so much blood before me on the earth. Behold, a son shall be born to you who shall be a man of rest. I will give him rest from all his surrounding enemies. For his name shall be <u>Solomon</u>, and I will give peace and quiet to Israel in his days. He shall build a house for my name. He shall be my son, and I will be his father, and I will establish his royal throne in Israel forever" (1 Chronicles 22:6-10).

So, scripture tells us that God loves Solomon and has selected him to build His house. Solomon will become the future king of Israel. As we explore Solomon's life, we will focus on his third son, Absalom, his fourth son, Adonijah, and his tenth son, **Solomon**.

Toward the end of his life, David is bedridden, has developed circulatory problems, and cannot keep warm even when they put covers over him. His attendants found **Abishag** (ab-is-shag), a beautiful Shunammite young woman and brought her to just lay with the king and provide body heat to keep him warm. She is later a large part of Solomon's story.

Absalom (ab-sa-lom) was the third son of King David, who eventually rebelled against his father and was killed during the Battle of Ephraim's Wood.

Adonijah (ad-o-ni-ja) was the fourth son of King David and is described as "a very handsome man," but he also misbehaved. Scripture indicates that the reason for Adonijah's misbehavior was that King David had neglected his discipline (1 Kings 1:6).

Solomon, the 10th son of *King David* (and *Bathsheba)* was given the name *"Jedidiah"* by God. *"The Lord loved him; and because the Lord loved him, he sent word through Nathan the prophet to name him Jedidiah"* (2 Samuel 12:25).

The name Jedidiah has a rich biblical history, means "beloved of God," and originates from the Hebrew name Yedidyah. The names Jedidiah and David are related in that the name David means "beloved." Solomon's life is described in 2 Samuel, 1 Kings, and 2 Chronicles.

Adonijah was older than Solomon; therefore, under normal circumstances, he would be in line before Solomon for the throne. But God promised that Solomon would be king. The tension between Adonijah and Solomon had been longstanding. When David was on his deathbed, like his brother Absalom, Adonijah gathered an army and presented himself to the people as king (2 Samuel 15).

Some influential men supported Adonijah's move, and they included **Joab**, captain of the Kings army, and **Abiathar** *(ab-a-thar)* the priest. But others opposed Adonijah's plans, including **Nathan** the prophet, **Zadok** (za-doc) the priest, and David's wife **Bathsheba** (1 Kings 1:8).

Adonijah had assembled his followers and offered many sacrifices as part of his coronation ceremony. When Nathan, the prophet, heard of these events, he encouraged Bathsheba to tell the ailing king about the situation. King David responded by ordering Solomon to be taken at once to Gihon and anointed by Nathan and Zadok as king. This happened, and Adonijah came before Solomon asking for clemency. Solomon promised him safety if he were found worthy, but he would be killed if evil were found in him. Adonijah was then allowed to return home.

But Adonijah was not through scheming. He later approached Bathsheba and implored her to ask Solomon for the hand of David's former nurse, *Abishag,* in marriage. Solomon became very angry and interpreted Adonijah's request as part of his brother's ongoing attempt to take over the kingdom of Israel.

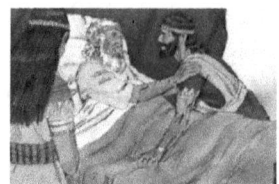 In those days, taking possession of a king's concubines was a declaration of one's right to the throne. 2 Samuel 16:22 states that this had been one of Absalom's methods when he led a coup against David. Since Abishag was considered part of David's harem, her marriage to Adonijah would have strengthened the usurper's claim to the throne. Solomon ordered Benaiah, one of David's mighty men, to kill Adonijah. King David's final instructions to Solomon had outlined the need for wisdom, justice, and adherence to God's commands.

> *"I am about to die, like all men must. But you are growing stronger and becoming a man. Now, carefully obey all the commands of the Lord your God. Carefully obey all his laws, commands, decisions, and agreements. Obey everything that is written in the Law of Moses. If you do this, you will be successful at whatever you do and wherever you go. And if you obey the Lord, he will keep his promise about me."* He said, *"If your sons carefully live the way I tell them, sincerely, with all their heart, the king of Israel will always be a man from your family."*

David also brought up a few grievances with certain men in his kingdom. He wanted **Joab** to be killed because Joab had previously killed two of David's allies, *Abner* and *Amasa*. David also wanted to punish **Shimei**, the man who cursed David and threw rocks at him when he fled Jerusalem during Absalom's rebellion (2 Samuel 16).

King David died and was buried in the City of David. He had reigned over Israel for 40 years; 7 years in Hebron and 33 years in Jerusalem. Solomon became king at the age of about twenty.

Solomon then banished Abiathar from the priesthood and sent him back to the fields in Anathoth. When Abiathar was banished from Jerusalem, therefore banished from serving as a priest, it fulfilled the word the Lord had spoken at Shiloh against the priestly house of Eli approximately 100 years earlier (1 Samuel 2:30-33).

Solomon then turned his attention to Joab, who had allied with Adonijah. Joab ran to the Tabernacle and took hold of the altar, hoping to find sanctuary, but Solomon instructed Benaiah to kill him. The king then assigned Benaiah, son of Jehoiada, over the army in Joab's position and replaced Abiathar with Zadok, the priest.

Then Solomon told Shimei, *"build a house in Jerusalem, live there, but do not go anywhere else. The day you leave and cross the Kidron Valley, you can be sure you will die; your blood will be on your own head."* Shimei agreed to these terms, but three years later, two of Shimei's slaves ran off to Gath, and Shimei went to retrieve them. After Solomon was told that Shimei had gone from Jerusalem to Gath, the king summoned Shimei and said that he had not kept his oath to the Lord and had not obeyed Solomon's command. Solomon had him killed.

A bit later, Solomon formed a marriage alliance with *Pharaoh*, the king of Egypt, and took Pharaoh's daughter to the city of David until he completed building his palace, the Temple of the Lord, and the wall around Jerusalem. Some scholars speculate that Solomon's wife was the daughter of *Pharaoh Shoshenq I*, and her name might have been *Nicaule* or *Tashere*. Although Pharaoh's daughter is not explicitly named in the Bible, she is described as marrying Solomon to solidify a political alliance between Israel and Egypt. This unique example shows the wealth and power of the Hebrew monarchy, as Pharaoh's daughters typically did not marry outside their own family.

At Gibeon, a city in Israel about five miles northwest of Jerusalem, God appeared in a vision, and Solomon said:

> *"Now, Lord my God, you have made your servant king in place of my father David. But I am only a little child and do not know how to carry out my duties. Your servant is here among the people you have chosen, a great people, too numerous to count or number. So give your servant a discerning heart to govern your people and to distinguish between right and wrong. For who is able to govern this great people of yours?"* (vv. 7–9)

Can you imagine the many things that Solomon could have asked for? However, he asked God for an understanding mind to govern God's people and to know the difference between good and evil. God was very pleased with Solomon's request. God said to him:

> *"Since you have asked for this and not for long life or wealth for yourself, nor have asked for the death of your enemies but for discernment in administering justice, I will do what you have asked. I will give you a wise and discerning heart, so that there will never have been anyone like you, nor will there ever be. Moreover, I will give you what you have not asked for—both wealth and honor—so that in your lifetime you will have no equal among kings. And if you walk in obedience to me and keep my decrees and commands as David your father did, I will give you a long life"* (vv. 11–15).

Solomon returned to Jerusalem, stood before the Ark of the Lord's Covenant, and sacrificed burnt and fellowship offerings.

Solomon had an extensive knowledge of the natural world. He spoke about plant life, from the cedar of Lebanon to the hyssop that grows from walls. He also talked about animals and birds, reptiles, and fish. Jewish tradition goes even further, crediting Solomon with the ability to converse in the language of every beast, fowl, fish, plant, and even demons. He understood their characteristics, medicinal properties, and moral lessons. Some legends even suggest that he could communicate directly with animals, receiving their wisdom and guidance (1 Kings 4:33).

Solomon's first recorded case as a judge came on a day when two harlot women who lived together and had recently given birth to sons came before him. During the night, one of the infants had tragically died, and the mother exchanged the dead child for the one that lived. Both mothers claimed that the living child was theirs.

Solomon used the divine wisdom that God had given him to test the women. He asked for a sword and proposed dividing the living child into two halves, giving each woman half of the child. The true mother immediately pleaded for the child's life, willing to give up her claim to save him. Solomon recognized her genuine love and awarded her custody of the child. And all Israel heard of this judgment, and they feared the king, because they saw that the wisdom of God was in him. The Lord granted Solomon wisdom far beyond that of other kings and blessed him with wealth, honor, and other pleasures.

Even the **Queen of Sheba** traveled many miles to see Solomon's glory and wisdom and exchange gifts.

"And when the queen of Sheba heard of the fame of Solomon concerning the name of the Lord, she came to prove him with hard questions."

Some think Sheba refers to the general area spanning South Arabia, the Horn of Africa, or Ethiopia. The Queen of Sheba ruled alone and was not enamored with the religions in her land.  She is also a figure in Jewish and Islamic traditions and was considered a woman of great wealth, beauty, and power.

The Queen of Sheba arrived at Jerusalem with a grand caravan loaded with spices, gold, and precious stones, and some scholars believe that she stayed and learned from

Solomon for six months. Solomon answered all her questions because nothing was too hard for the king to explain to her. She was overwhelmed with Solomon's wisdom, the palace he had built, and the Temple of the Lord.

> She said, "*Praise be to the Lord your God, who has delighted in you and placed you on the throne of Israel. Because of the Lord's eternal love for Israel, he has made you king to maintain justice and righteousness.*"

Before leaving, she gave the king 120 talents of gold (roughly 8,995 pounds worth approximately $305 million U.S. dollars), large quantities of spices, and precious stones. Then she left and returned with her retinue to her own country.

Fact or fiction? Sources outside the Bible suggest that the Queen of Sheba was named **Makeda** and conceived a child secretly with King Solomon, **Menilek I** (also Menelik I). The child became the legendary first Emperor of Ethiopia and inaugurated the Solomonic dynasty of Ethiopia in the 10th century BC. Again, this is open to speculation.

King Solomon was very wealthy; the gold he received yearly was 666 talents (21 tons). That did not include the revenue from merchants, traders, Arabian kings, the governors of the territories, or the heavy tax placed on the people to support his many building projects. On top of all these riches, he received immense wealth from his father David. Could the number 666 symbolize Solomon's fall from wisdom and righteousness, as he turned away from God's commands?

At one point, Solomon made a great ivory throne and overlaid it with gold. On both sides of the seat were armrests, with a lion standing beside each. Twelve lions stood on the six steps, one at either end of each step. All of Solomon's drinking vessels were pure gold. He also had a fleet of trading ships at sea, along with the ships of Hiram, the king of Tyre. Once every three years, they returned, carrying gold, silver, ivory, apes, and baboons. Hiram was an ally of the Israelite King David and became a friend of King Solomon (2 Samuel, 1 Kings, and 1 Chronicles). Hiram was very pleased to hear that Solomon had taken David's place and said, *"Blessed be the LORD this day, for He has given David a wise son over this great people!"*

When Solomon asked for help in building a temple and a new palace, projects which took him twenty years to complete, Hiram sent him cedar and cypress wood from the forests of Lebanon, all the gold he needed, and all the skilled workmen necessary for erecting and furnishing the buildings. In return, Solomon supplied him with twenty cities in the land of Galilee, food for his household, gifts, and they also engaged together in Mediterranean and Red Sea trading voyages. When Solomon built a fleet of ships at Ezion-geber, on the shore of the Red Sea, Hiram sent him experienced seamen to work with Solomon's men on the ships.

King Solomon also had fourteen hundred chariots and twelve thousand horsemen. He exceeded all the kings of the earth for riches and wisdom, and all the earth sought to hear the wisdom of Solomon, which God had put in his heart. However, as wealthy and wise as King Solomon was, he had a big problem. He loved many foreign women, including Moabites, Ammonites, Edomites, Sidonians, and Hittites. The Lord had told the Israelites, *"You must not intermarry with them, because they will surely turn your hearts after their gods."*

The dictionary defines *polygamy* as a "state of marriage to many spouses." However, in Solomon's case, it was carried out on a scale corresponding to the magnificence of his kingdom. It was probably used as a political object of alliance with neighboring kings. 1 Kings 11:3 states that he had 700 wives and 300 concubines. The large number and array of his mistresses were to enhance his state and renown.

As he exceeded other kings in glory, wisdom, and power, he also exceeded them in armies, chariots, horses, and the number of wives. This large harem was likely made up of heathen women who practiced their special religious observances without the help of the priests. Solomon built temples for their foreign worship. Solomon's wives indeed led him astray.

As Solomon grew older, the wives turned his heart after other gods, and his heart was not entirely devoted to the Lord his God. Solomon, by degrees, became a public worshipper of abominable idols and lost his relish for true wisdom. He followed *Ashtoreth*, the goddess of the Sidonians. He even built a high place of worship on a hill east of Jerusalem for Chemosh, the detestable god of Moab, and for Molek, the detestable god of the Ammonites. He did the same for all his foreign wives, who burned incense and offered sacrifices to their gods. The Lord was angry with Solomon because his heart had turned away from Him.

He had forbidden Solomon to follow other gods, yet Solomon did not keep the Lord's command. But because of the Lord's love for David, the Lord said:

"Since this is your attitude and you have not kept my covenant and my decrees, which I commanded you, I will most certainly tear the kingdom away from you and give it to one of your subordinates. "Nevertheless, for the sake of David your father, I will not do it during your lifetime. I will tear it out of the hand of your son. Yet I will not tear the whole kingdom from him, but will give him one tribe for the sake of David my servant and for the sake of Jerusalem, which I have chosen."

In addition to the consequences of his disobedience, God raised adversaries against Solomon. One such adversary was **Hadad the Edomite**, who belonged to the king's seed in Edom. When David was fighting with Edom, he had killed all the men in Edom except for a young boy named Hadad, who had fled to Egypt. Hadad's presence posed a challenge to Solomon's reign and stability.

God raised another adversary against Solomon: **Rezon, son of Eliada**, who had fled from his master, Hadadezer, king of Zobah. After David destroyed Zobah's army, Rezon became the leader of the men, and they all went to Damascus, where they settled and took control. Rezon was Israel's adversary as long as Solomon lived.

And there were other problems besides Hadad and Rezon. One of Solomon's officials, **Jeroboam son of Nebat** (jer-a-bo-am), also rebelled against the king. When Solomon saw how well Jeroboam did his work, he put him in charge of the whole labor force of the tribes of Joseph.

As Jeroboam was leaving Jerusalem, **Ahijah the prophet of Shiloh** (a-hi-ja) met him on the way, wearing a new cloak. Ahijah took hold of the new cloak he was wearing and tore it into twelve pieces. He then told Jeroboam, *"Take ten pieces for yourself, for this is what the LORD, the God of Israel, says: "See, I am going to tear the kingdom out of Solomon's hand and give you ten tribes. But for the sake of my servant David and the city of Jerusalem, which I have chosen out of all the tribes of Israel, he will have one tribe."*

Ahijah told Jeroboam that if he followed the Lord and was faithful to the Law, he would have God's promise: *"I will build you a dynasty as enduring as the one I built for David and will give Israel to you"* (verse 38). After Ahijah's prophecy, Solomon tried to kill Jeroboam for his rebellion, but Jeroboam fled safely to Egypt.

Sidenote: Ahijah had torn the garment into 12 pieces, giving 10 to Jeroboam. This symbolic action represents how the Lord will make Jeroboam king over ten of the tribes of Israel. One piece is reserved for Solomon—the tribe of Judah, which stays under the rule of the House of David. So, what tribe does the 12th piece represent? The twelfth piece is not explicitly mentioned in the text. However, some suggest that it represents the tribe of Levi, which did not receive a territorial inheritance but instead served as priests for all the other eleven tribes. Some scholars say Benjamin, or could it be Simeon?

When Solomon passed away, Jeroboam returned to warn Solomon's son **Rehoboam** (ray-o-bow-am) to lighten the load of labor imposed upon the people of Israel (1 Kings 12:4).

Rehoboam refused and angrily promised to increase the load. In response, the people of Israel revolted against Rehoboam, and everything happened as Ahijah had prophesied. The kingdom split; Jeroboam became king over most tribes, the northern kingdom of Israel, and David's descendants were left with the southern kingdom of Judah. But Jeroboam was not the king Israel needed.

Jeroboam continued to publicize idol worship and led the people astray. This angered the Lord, and He brought disaster upon the house of Jeroboam. This prophecy was fulfilled with the destruction of Jeroboam's entire family at the hands of King Baasha. All of this would be done because Solomon had not obeyed God.

Other Interesting Items:

I suppose the questions need to be asked: *If Solomon was the wisest of the wise, how could he have made these unwise decisions of marrying foreign wives and following them into idolatry? How far should one go when making concessions to a spouse who is not of one's faith? If multiple religions exist, which religion would be prevalent in the home?*

Solomon allowed himself to be swayed away from his faith by his wives, showing a preoccupation with temporal over spiritual responsibilities. We will probably never know for sure why Solomon made these unwise decisions.

Many things in the life of King Solomon point to the fact that the Lord indeed loved him. Under Solomon's rule, Israel enjoyed a time of great prosperity, and his kingdom was extended to its largest geographical capacity with victories over the Philistines, Moabites, Ammonites, and Edomites.

The crowning achievement of King Solomon's reign was the erection of a magnificent temple in Jerusalem, often called **Solomon's Temple** or the **First Temple**. Solomon built the

House of the Lord in Jerusalem on Mount Moriah, where the Lord had appeared to his father, David. The site was originally a threshing floor David had bought from Araunah the Jebusite (2 Samuel 24:18-25; 2 Chronicles 3:1). A fascinating fact concerning the building of the temple was that there was no noise from the construction. The material was prepared at a quarry before being brought to the building site.

The Scripture indicates that the inside ceiling of Solomon's temple was 180 feet long, 90 feet wide, and 50 feet high. The highest point on the temple was about 20 stories or 207 feet tall. The construction and dedication of Solomon's temple are described in 1 Kings 6:1-38 and chapters 7-8. This temple was destroyed by the Babylonians some 400 years later.

About 70 years after this, a second temple, **Herod's Temple,** was completed on the same site. The Romans destroyed this temple in AD 70 during the siege of Jerusalem, and only a small part of the retaining wall remains, known as *"The Wailing Wall."*

Solomon wrote the Song of Solomon, the Book of Ecclesiastes, and much of the Book of Proverbs. The Song of Solomon is one of 1,005 songs that Solomon wrote. It is a lyric poem written to extol the virtues of love between a husband and his wife (1 Kings 4:32). The poem presents marriage as God's design. A man and woman are to live together within the context of marriage, loving each other spiritually, emotionally, and physically.

The Book of Ecclesiastes is essentially an autobiographical narrative, with the central theme being humanity's fruitless quest for contentment. Although some contest Solomon's authorship of Ecclesiastes, many of the author's descriptions align perfectly with Solomon. The Book of Proverbs is a compilation of 3000 practical life wisdoms, mostly presented in short, memorable statements.

Did Solomon ever repent for his sins? God said, *"I have chosen him to be my son, and I will be his father"* (1 Chronicles 28:6). King Solomon sinned greatly against the Lord, marrying pagan wives, building pagan altars for them, and even participating in pagan worship himself. The book of Ecclesiastes is a dark study of a life lived apart from God.

So, the ultimate answer to whether Solomon was saved rests with God, not us. Solomon's writings clearly speak of a man who had a personal relationship with God and knew firsthand the folly of living without God. Solomon died a shell of a man—empty, hopeless, and full of regret.

> *"When I surveyed all that my hands had done and what I had toiled to achieve, everything was meaningless, a chasing after the wind; nothing was gained under the sun."*

> *"For the Lord watches over the way of the righteous, but the way of the wicked leads to destruction."*

We end this story with the death of King Solomon. His reign is conventionally dated from about 970 BC to 931 BC. He died of natural causes and was buried in the City of David. Solomon was the third and last king of the united kingdom of Israel, following King Saul and King David. He reigned for 40 years during one of the most prosperous periods in Israel's history, often called the *"Golden Age"* of Israel.

Solomon's life offers many lessons. If we seek God with all of our heart, He will be found, and He will honor those who honor Him.

> *"The fear of the LORD is the beginning of knowledge, but fools despise wisdom and instruction."*
> — (Proverbs 1:7)

The Story of Elijah

Elijah was a prophet and miracle worker who lived in the northern kingdom of Israel during the reign of the Israelite Kings Ahab, Ahaziah, and Jehoram. He defended the worship of the *Hebrew deity **Yahweh*** over that of the *Canaanite and Phoenician deity **Baal***. He also emphasized monotheism (the belief in the existence of one true God) and lived during times of wicked rulers. Elijah's story is told in 1 Kings 17–19; 2 Kings 1–2; Malachi; Hebrews; and 2 Chronicles and is mentioned in the New Testament in Luke; Romans; James; and Revelation.

Elijah was born of the tribe of **Aaron** in 900 BCE in the village of Tishbe (*or Thisbe*), in Gilead, east of the Jordan River. His father's name was **Savah**, but his mother's identity was not revealed. The name Elijah comes from the Bible's Old Testament and stems from a Hebrew expression signifying, "*Jehovah is my God*," and has been variously translated as "*My God is the Lord.*"

Elijah's life was filled with turmoil. At times he was bold and decisive, and at other times fearful and tentative. It is said that during his life, Elijah knew both the power of God and the depths of depression.

During this time, the Jewish kingdom was divided into two unequal parts: the ***kingdom of Judah***, consisting of the tribes of Judah and Benjamin, with its capital in Jerusalem, and the ***kingdom of Israel***, consisting of the remaining ten tribes, with its capital in Samaria (modern-day Sebastia).

Our story begins with Elijah telling King Ahab, "*As the Lord, the God of Israel, lives, whom I serve, there will be neither dew nor rain in the next few years except at my word*" (1st Kings Chapter 17).

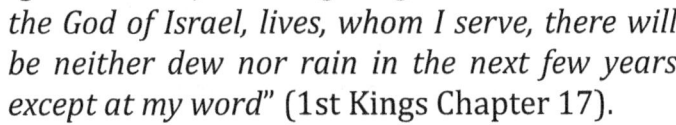

God has brought a drought upon the entire land as a consequence for the nation's rampant idolatry, led by the evil royal couple **King Ahab and Queen Jezebel.** God tells Elijah to go to the brook of

Cherith, where God commanded the ravens to bring Elijah bread and flesh each day. The drought and famine continued, and in time the brook dried up. God then told Elijah to go to the city of **Zarephath** (a town outside of Israel), where a widow woman would give him food and water.

Elijah met the woman at the city gate and asked her for food and water. She replied that she only had a handful of meal (flour) in a barrel, and a little oil in a cruse (jug), and it was barely enough for her and her son. She was gathering sticks so that she could prepare a last meal for her and her son, because they would surely die of starvation.

Elijah told her to prepare the food, and that she would continue to have food until the Lord sends rain upon the earth. She had faith in Elijah's words and made the meal. The Lord then provided food enough for Elijah, the woman, and her son, and miraculously, the widow's barrel of meal and jar of oil never ran out (1 Kings 17:8-16).

Elijah stayed there for some time, living in an upper room of the widow's house. Later, the son became sick and died, and she said unto Elijah, *"What have I to do with thee, O thou man of God? art thou come unto me to call my sin to remembrance, and to slay my son?"* The widow blamed Elijah for his death—she assumed God was judging her for her sin.

Elijah took the son up into the loft where he slept and laid the boy on the bed. Elijah then cried to God: *"Lord my God, let this boy's life return to him!"* The Lord heard his plea, and the child was revived and returned to his mother. When the woman saw this, she said, *"Now I know that you are a man of God and that the word of the Lord from your mouth is the truth."*

The New Testament also mentions this account in Luke 4:25-26. Early in His ministry, **Jesus** was speaking in the synagogue of His hometown, Nazareth, and said, *"In truth, I tell you, there were many widows in Israel in the days of Elijah, when the heavens were shut up three years and six months, and a great famine came over all the land, and Elijah was sent to none of them but only to Zarephath, in the land of Sidon, to a woman who was a widow."*

Jesus' point was that no prophet is accepted in his hometown. Just as Elijah found more faith outside of Israel than within it, Jesus found little faith in His boyhood home.

God spoke to Elijah in the third year of the drought and told him to go talk to **King Ahab**. On his way, Elijah met **Obadiah**, a righteous man who was Ahab's palace administrator. Earlier, Obadiah had hidden and fed 100 prophets of God when Jezebel, Ahab's wife, tried to kill them. Elijah met with King Ahab and told him that the drought was caused by the king abandoning God's commands and following the god Baal.

Elijah told Ahab to gather the people of Israel, the 450 prophets of Baal, and the 400 prophets of Asherah, another false Canaanite deity, and to meet him at *Mount Carmel*. And they did. Elijah told the people they could choose to serve God or idols, but they couldn't choose both.

The people were silent, and **Elijah then challenged the prophets of Baal to a test**. Elijah and the prophets of Baal would each build an altar and put a bull on it for sacrifice. Then they would pray and cry to their god to bring fire from heaven to the altar sacrifice. The God who answered with fire from the sky would be considered the true God.

Baal's prophets went first, and they cried out to Baal from morning until noon, but nothing happened. Elijah mocked them, and they shouted louder and slashed themselves with swords and spears, as was their custom, until their blood flowed. They continued their frantic praying until the time for the evening sacrifice.

When it was Elijah's turn, he asked that 12 jars of water be poured on his wood and into the trench dug around the altar. The water soaked the sacrifice, the wood, and filled the trench. Elijah then prayed, *"Lord, the God of Abraham, Isaac and Israel, let it be known today that you are God in Israel and that I am your servant and have done all these things at your command. Answer me, Lord, answer me, so these people will know that you, Lord, are God, and that you are turning their hearts back again."*

Fire fell from heaven and consumed the bull, wood, stones, and even the remaining water in the trench surrounding the altar. The people of Israel bowed down and declared the Lord as God. After this, Elijah and the people killed all of the 450 false prophets of Baal, in compliance with God's command (Deuteronomy 13:5).

> *"And that prophet, or that dreamer of dreams, shall be put to death; because he hath spoken to turn you away from the Lord your God, which brought you out of the land of Egypt, and redeemed you out of the house of bondage, to thrust thee out of the way which the Lord thy God commanded thee to walk in. So shalt thou put the evil away from the midst of thee."*

While on top of Mount Carmel, Elijah prayed for rain; the sky became dark and heavy rain fell on Israel (1 Kings 18:41-46).

King Ahab told his wife, Jezebel, of God's majestic display of power, and instead of turning to God, **Jezebel vowed to kill Elijah**. Elijah was made aware of this, and he fled a day's journey into the wilderness and sat down under a juniper tree.

Here, he wanted to die and said to the Lord, *"O Lord, take away my life; for I am not better than my fathers."* The prophet's depression reached its lowest point here. Jezebel threatened him, leaving him weary and alone in the desert. Elijah sees no reason to succeed when all the prophets before him have failed.

That night as he slept, an angel touched him and told him to rise and eat. The angel had provided a cake baked on the coals, and a cruse (small earthen vessel or flask) of water. After he had eaten, the angel told Elijah to prepare for a long journey of forty days and forty nights to Mt. Horeb (Mt. Sinai).

While staying in a cave on Mt. Horeb, the word of the Lord came to him and said, *"What doest thou here, Elijah?"* Elijah replied, *"I have been very jealous for the Lord God of hosts: because the children of Israel have forsaken thy covenant, thrown down thine altars, and slain thy prophets with the sword; and I, even I only, am left; and they seek my life, to take it away."*

God said, *"Go forth, and stand upon the mount before the Lord."* The Lord then passed by, and a great and strong wind broke the rocks, but the Lord was not in the wind. Then an earthquake and then a fire occurred, but the Lord was not in the earthquake or the fire. But then Elijah heard a small voice once again say, *"What doest thou here, Elijah?"*

Perhaps it is best to view this as God speaking to the despondent Elijah tenderly instead of with all His majestic power. God is revealing Himself to Elijah differently than what Elijah had previously known.

Then the Lord told Elijah to go to the *Desert of Damascus* and anoint **Hazael** (hi-zael) to be the king over Syria, **Jehu** (ja-who) the son of Nimshi, to be king over Israel, and **Elisha** (e-li-sa) the son of Shaphat of Abel-meholah, to be the prophet in your place.

Jehu would slay those unfaithful in Israel who escaped the sword of Hazael, and Elisha would slay those who escaped the sword of Jehu. The Lord had 7,000 loyal men in Israel who had not bowed to Baal.

Elijah left and found **Elisha** plowing with twelve yokes of oxen. He told Elisha that he was God's choice as a prophet, and that he was to follow Elijah. Elisha had a meal with his family and then followed Elijah. He became Elijah's assistant and the two continued to deal with Ahab and Jezebel, as well as Ahab's son and successor, Ahaziah.

I now go to the second book of Kings, which takes place after the death of King Ahab. Ahab's son **Ahaziah** (A-ha-zi-a) fell through a lattice in his upper chamber in Samaria. He then got very ill and sent his officials to ask **Baalzebub, the god of Ekron**, if he'd recover from this illness.

The angel of the Lord told Elijah to meet the king's messengers and say unto them, *"Forasmuch as thou hast sent messengers to enquire of Baalzebub the god of Ekron, is it not because there is no God in Israel to enquire of his word?"*

Elijah told the men that Ahaziah would not recover but would die. Ahaziah chose to ask the false gods of Ekron instead of the Lord God of Israel for help. The messengers relayed this message back to Ahaziah. When he heard this, Ahaziah asked who the man who said this was. They answered, "He *had a garment of hair and had a leather belt around his waist.*" Ahaziah said, "It is Elijah the Tishbite."

Ahaziah then sent groups of 50 men and a captain to detain Elijah so he could not tell him he would die. They found Elijah on a hill and told him to come down. Elijah replied to the captain, "*If I be a man of God, then let fire come down from heaven, and consume thee and thy fifty.*"

And fire came down from heaven and consumed him and his fifty. Another captain and another group of 50 men came to get Elijah, and he replied, "*If I be a man of God, let fire come down from heaven, and consume thee and thy fifty.*" And the fire of God came down from heaven and consumed him and his fifty.

Then a third captain and another fifty men approached, but this time the captain fell to his knees before Elijah and begged Elijah to spare their lives. Elijah and the captain then went to see the ailing king. Elijah told Ahaziah face to face that he would die, and later he died. Jehoram, his brother, ruled in his place because Ahaziah had no children.

Elijah and Elisha now journey to Bethel, Jericho, and Jordan. At each place, the sons of the prophets said to Elisha, "*Knowest thou that the Lord will take away thy master from thy head today? And he said, Yea, I know it; hold ye your peace.*"

And fifty men of the sons of the prophets went to the Jordan River to see the divine transition of prophetic authority from Elijah to Elisha.

Elijah took his cloak, rolled it up, and hit the water with it. The water divided, and the two men went across on dry ground. Elijah asked Elisha what he could do for him before he was taken away, and Elisha said, "*I pray thee, let a double portion of thy spirit be upon me.*"

Elijah said that Elisha had asked a hard thing, but let it be so. This request asked that Elisha be doubly blessed in his life and ministry. Interestingly, Scripture records exactly twice as many miracles through Elisha (16 miracles) as took place through Elijah (8 miracles). However, some scholars have disputed these numbers.

As they walked and talked, a chariot and horses of fire appeared. Rather than die a natural death, Elijah was taken to heaven in the whirlwind (2 Kings 2:1-11). It is thought that this mode of transportation God chose for Elijah holds some important symbolism. The horses speak of power and speed; the chariot speaks of protection and triumph; the whole being "of fire" speaks of glory. God took His servant speedily, triumphantly into the glories of heaven, guarding his soul all the way.

The prophet who had shown such fiery zeal for God, and who had literally called down fire from heaven several times, was now taken to heaven in fire. Elisha then took Elijah's cloak and returned to the Jordan River. He hit the water with the cloak and said, *"Where is the Lord God of Elijah? and when he also had smitten the waters, they parted hither and thither: and Elisha went over."* The sons of the prophets saw all of this and knew that the spirit of Elijah rested on Elisha.

The spirit and power of Elijah marked John the Baptist's ministry. *"And he will go on before the Lord, in the spirit and power of Elijah, to turn the hearts of the parents to their children and the disobedient to the wisdom of the righteous–to make ready a people prepared for the Lord"* (Luke 1:17).

At His transfiguration, **Jesus** presented His three closest disciples (Peter, James, and John) with a stunning sneak preview of His resplendent glory: "His face shone like the sun, and his clothes became as white as the light. Just then there appeared before them **Moses and Elijah**, talking with Jesus" (Matthew 17:2-3). The presence of Moses and Elijah, who respectively stand for the Law and the Prophets, was to signal the arrival of their long-awaited Messiah.

The Bible describes two individuals who will help carry out God's work during the Tribulation (Revelation 11:3-12). Nowhere does the Bible identify these two witnesses by name, although people have speculated that they could be *Moses and Elijah* or *Enoch and Elijah*.

The Book of Daniel

The Book of Daniel contains prophecies and historical accounts of the Israelites' exile to Babylon. The book is part of the Old Testament, and the theme of the book  is very simple: God is sovereign. Some things discussed in the Book of Daniel are also referenced in the **Book of Revelation**. Daniel reveals the first coming of Jesus, his death, and the destruction of Israel, Jerusalem, and the Temple. Revelation speaks of events after these, plus an outline of things related to the Second Coming of Jesus. Many end-time details are presented. Some have said that Daniel did not write the book, but his writing is verified in Daniel 12:4:

"But thou, O Daniel, shut up the words, and seal the book, even to the time of the end: many shall run to and fro, and knowledge shall be increased."

Jesus said, *"So when you see standing in the holy place "the abomination that causes desolation, spoken of through the prophet Daniel—let the reader understand"* (Matthew 24:15).

To offer a bit of history, God had made a covenant with Abraham, saying that the land would be given to him and his descendants, and he would be a blessing to others. God said He would bless nations through Abraham's children and curse those who curse him. His sons Issac, Jacob, and Joseph all have essential stories in the Bible. Keep in mind that later, when Moses led the Hebrews out of Egypt to the Promised Land, God promised this land to them in the Mosaic Covenant. God would continue to bless them if they kept His laws. The people agreed, but few followed God's commandments by Daniel's time, and many worshiped idols.

Chapter 1: This chapter teaches us that faithfulness to God often comes with trials, but it is met with divine favor and wisdom. Despite being in a foreign land under oppressive circumstances, Daniel and his friends remain firm in their convictions. Their obedience protects and sets them apart, showing God's power and faithfulness. Our story begins in 605 BC. This is the third year of the reign of **King Jehoiakim of Judah.** The conquering **King of Babylon, Nebuchadnezzar,** and his army captured Jerusalem and took many hostages back to Babylon. Among the hostages are **Daniel, Hananiah** (han-a-niah), **Mishael** (me-shael), and **Azariah** (az-a-riah); young men probably 11-15 years of age.

These young men are very well thought of and go into a three-year training program to serve in the king's court. The program was monitored by Ashpenaz, the chief of his court officials, and their names were changed; Daniel to **Belteshazzar,** Hananiah to **Shadrach**, Mishael to **Meshach,** and Azariah to **Abednego**.

The Hebrew name signified ***Monotheism***—only one God—while the Babylonian name signified more than one God. Babylonia mainly focused on the god Marduk, who was the national god of the Babylonian empire. The God of Daniel is consistently called the Most High God—**Jehovah** (Isaiah 42:8).

During their training, Daniel convinced Ashpenaz that they should not eat the royal food that would offend their God because it had probably been offered to the Babylonian idols. They would eat only vegetables and grain, and drink only water. The request was granted, and after 10 days, the group was tested and was better nourished than any of the young men who ate the royal food. God had given this group of young men unusual knowledge and understanding, and Daniel, with God's assistance, could understand dreams and visions.

Chapter 2: 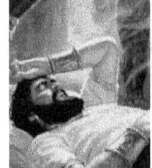 King Nebuchadnezzar has a troubling dream, and he calls all his wise astrologers, etc., to reveal what the dream was and what it meant. If they could not, they would all die, including Daniel and his companions. However, no astrologer could interpret the dream without knowing it first. Daniel was made aware of the king's demand by the King's Captain Arioch and asked for one day to pray and ask God for help. After much prayer by Daniel and his team, God gave Daniel the answer to the dream. Daniel ensured the king knew that the interpretation came from God, not from him.

"The dream featured a huge, glorious statue of a man. Its head was "made of pure gold, its chest and arms of silver, its belly and thighs of bronze, its legs of iron, its feet partly of iron and partly of baked clay. Then a rock cut "not by human hands" hit the foot of the statue, and the whole image "became like chaff on a threshing floor," while the rock "became a huge mountain and filled the whole earth."

Daniel interpreted the dream to the King as follows:

Head of gold: **Babylon**

Chest of silver: **Medes and Persians**

Belly and thighs of bronze: **Greece**

Legs of iron: **Rome**

Feet partially of iron and clay: **A divided and weak kingdom**. (Some think that this empire is yet to come and represents the kingdom of the Antichrist—a "revived Roman Empire?")

Rock: **A symbol of Jesus and the future everlasting kingdom that would break all other kingdoms.**

Upon hearing this, the king fell on his face and said, *"Truly, your God is God of gods and Lord of kings, and a revealer of mysteries, for you have been able to reveal this mystery."* He then promoted Daniel and made him chief administrator over all the wise men, and Daniel's companions were also rewarded. Keep in mind that Daniel is probably still a teenager or in his early 20s.

Chapter 3: It is thought that approximately 16-20 years have passed, and the arrogant, prideful, and demanding Nebuchadnezzar is still King, and the jealous wise men are still serving under Daniel. The king has a gold statue made of himself that was (90 feet high x 9 feet wide), and places it southeast of Babylon in the Plain of Dura.

At the sound of music, everyone is expected to bow and worship the statue or die a fiery death in a furnace. Daniel's three friends refused to worship the idol, even though the king gave them another chance to "bow and worship." They told the king that they serve a greater God.

The furnace was heated to seven times its normal temperature, and the three men were cast into the fire. The fire was so hot that it killed the men putting Daniel's friends into it. But suddenly, the king saw four men walking in the fire, and none were being burned. The king said the fourth looked like a god (perhaps a *"Christophany,"* a pre-incarnate appearance of Christ).

When the king removed the three men from the fire, they had no burns and no smell of smoke. Once again, King Nebuchadnezzar praised their God and promoted the three men. The Bible does not say where Daniel was during this timeframe.

*In theology, a *"theophany"* is a biblical manifestation of God in a tangible form, a visible appearance, particularly in the Old Testament. An example is God's appearance to Moses in a burning bush. A *"Christophany"* refers to a manifestation of Jesus in a tangible form, often seen as a pre-incarnate appearance of Christ, such as during the transfiguration when Jesus reveals His divine nature.

Chapter 4: King Nebuchadnezzar tells how he learned a lesson of God's sovereignty and humbled himself before the true God. Daniel has been in Babylon for 40-plus years and is well past 50 years old. The king has a second dream that terrifies him, and once again, the wise men cannot interpret it. Daniel is called, and the dream consisted of "a **strong tree of great height in the midst of the earth.**" The tree grew, leaves and fruit were abundant, and all flesh was fed from it. But then he saw a watcher and a holy one (both are angels), and it is said that the tree would be chopped down. The stump and roots, however, would be left but bound with a band of iron and bronze. This was the decree of the Most High.

The king would live with the animals and be given the mind of an animal until seven times (7 years) pass. This would happen so that he would know that the Most High is sovereign over all kingdoms on earth. He can give empires to anyone he wishes and set the lowest of people over them.

Daniel was concerned about telling the king the interpretation since it concerned how the king would be judged. The dream warned the king to humble himself and recognize that his power, wealth, and influence were from God, not of his own making. He would lose his kingdom and be a wild creature for seven years but would regain his knowledge and kingdom when he stated that God was the sovereign ruler of everything. Daniel told the king to repent of his pride, but he did not listen.

Twelve months passed, and the king was walking on the roof of the royal palace of Babylon when he said, *"Is not this the great Babylon I have built as the royal residence, by my mighty power and for the glory of my majesty?"*

Immediately, what had been said about Nebuchadnezzar in the dream was fulfilled. He was driven away from people and ate grass like an ox. His body was drenched with the dew of heaven until his hair grew like the feathers of an eagle and his nails like the claws of a bird. Nebuchadnezzar raised his eyes toward heaven at the end of seven years, and his sanity and kingdom were restored. He praised the Most High and honored and glorified the God of Daniel, who lives forever.

Chapter 5: Here, we read about a mysterious supernatural event in the grand palace of King Belshazzar, whose name means "Bel protect the king." Bel was a Babylonian god. Twenty years have passed since King Nebuchadnezzar's death, and his grandson Belshazzar is the reigning king. Babylonian life is a grand party—live for pleasure today! To see what God thought of these people, read Isaiah 47.

A great drunken feast is held, and Belshazzar commands that the gold and silver vessels that King Nebuchadnezzar took from the Jerusalem Temple of God be brought so that wine can be drunk from them as the group praises their idols. This happens even as the **Medo-Persian army** is outside the walls of Babylon.

As they commit this sacrilege, the fingers of a man's hand suddenly appear and a message is written on the wall: **Mene, Mene, Tekel, Upharsin**. The king 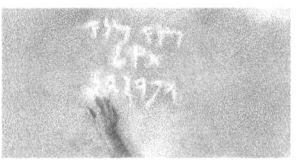 said the one who could interpret the words would be clothed in purple, have a gold chain around their neck, and would be made the third ruler in the kingdom. But once again, none of the king's wise men could interpret the vision.

The queen reminded Belshazzar of Daniel interpreting dreams in the past years. Daniel was summoned. He was not fond of the king, but said he would interpret. But first, Daniel reminded Belshazzar that God had given King Nebuchadnezzar sovereignty, greatness, glory, and splendor, but He also humbled the king. He reminded Belshazzar that God can put kings in place or remove them. But you, Belshazzar, did not honor the God who holds your life and all your ways in his hand. Therefore, he sent the hand that wrote the inscription. Daniel said the interpretation was:

> **Mene, Mene**: God has numbered your kingdom and finished it.

Tekel: You have been weighed in the balance and found guilty.

Upharsin: Your kingdom has been divided between the Medes and Persians. That night, Belshazzar, the last King of Babylon, was slain.

The term "the handwriting is on the wall" today usually references "impending doom" or "something bad is getting ready to happen."

Keep in mind that no one thought the city of Babylon could be captured since it was basically an armed fortress. The city had great walls, manned towers on top of them, and a moat surrounding it filled with water. A second wall was inside, and land there was used for farming. The Euphrates River flowed under the walls, providing a year-round drinking and farming water supply.

However, **Cyrus the Great** diverted the Euphrates River upstream, lowering the water level, which allowed his men to enter under the walls. Then, they lowered the drawbridges, allowing the army to attack the city. Darius the Mede took over the kingdom at the age of sixty-two.

Chapter 6: This chapter beautifully illustrates the victory of unwavering faith and righteousness over deceit and danger. Amidst adversity, Daniel's devotion to God does not waver, proving that steadfast faith can lead to divine intervention and justice when faced with trials. It reaffirms God's power, invincibility, and protective hand over those who serve Him faithfully. So now we are approaching the story that everyone loves—**Daniel and the lion's den**.

Darius the Mede is now King and has set up 120 satraps (provinces) with Daniel as one of the three governors that are in command. Daniel does an exceptional job, and the king plans to set him over the kingdom. Hearing this, the jealous administrators and provincial governors tried to find ways to accuse Daniel of corruption in his government affairs, but they could not. So, these deceitful people asked the king to issue and enforce an edict stating that anyone who prays to any god or human being other than the king during the next thirty days would be thrown into the lions' den. The edict could not be repealed once issued, based on the law of the Medes and Persians. King Darius put the decree into writing.

It's interesting that once Daniel heard of the decree, he went home to his upstairs room, opened his window toward Jerusalem, and prayed. Three times each day, he got down on his knees and prayed, giving thanks to his God, just as he had done before the decree.

The evil group that had instigated the decree reminded the king that anyone who prayed to any god or human being except the king during the next thirty days would be thrown into the lion's den. Then, they told the king that Daniel had violated the decree. The king was distressed, but at this point, nothing could be done to save Daniel.

Daniel was thrown into the lion's den, and a stone was placed over its mouth. The king sealed the stone with his signet ring. The king then spent a sleepless night worrying about his friend Daniel's faith. The king returned early the next morning and found that Daniel was safe, and that God had sent his angel to shut the mouths of the lions.

Daniel said the beasts had not harmed him because he had been found innocent in God's and the king's eyes. The king was overjoyed and had Daniel lifted out of the den. The men who had falsely accused Daniel were brought in and thrown into the lions' den, along with their wives and children. King Darius then wrote to all the nations and peoples of every language on earth, praising the God of Daniel.

Chapter 7: We read about Daniel's vision of four beasts coming out of the sea, representing four empires that oppress God's people. In the first year of Belshazzar, the king of Babylon, Daniel had a night dream. In this vision, he saw the four winds of heaven churning up the great sea and four great beasts, each different from the others, coming up out of the sea.

The first beast was like a **lion**, and it had the wings of an eagle until its wings were torn off and it stood on two feet like a human being. The mind of a human was given to it. The second beast looked like a **bear**. It was raised up on one of its sides, and it had three ribs in its mouth between its teeth and was told to get up and eat your fill of flesh! The third beast looked like a **leopard**, with four wings on its back and four heads, and was given authority to rule. The fourth beast was terrifying, frightening, and very powerful. It had **large iron teeth**, and it crushed and devoured its victims and trampled them underfoot. It was different from all the former beasts, and **it had ten horns and another little horn.** This horn had eyes like the eyes of a human being and a mouth that talked boastfully as he spoke against the Most High. While Daniel was thinking about the horns, another little horn came up among them; and three of the first horns were uprooted before it.

The vision then shifts to a heavenly court with the ***Ancient of Days*** (God) presiding. There is a flaming throne with wheels of fire, and God's hair and clothing are as white as snow. The flaming throne may symbolize judgment, and the white hair and title "Ancient" may indicate that God existed before time began.

A river of fire was flowing before him, and many thousands stood before Him. The court was seated, and the books were opened. The court passes judgment on the fourth beast, slaying it and throwing its body into the burning fire. The other beasts were stripped of their authority but allowed to live for a time. Then, the ***Son of Man*** (Jesus) approached God and was given dominion, glory, and an everlasting kingdom that will never pass away.

The four beasts are future kingdoms on earth, and the fourth beast will be different and vicious. It will devour the world, and the ten horns are ten kings who will come from this kingdom. After them, another different king will rise, and he will subdue the other three kings. This king will speak against God, persecute his holy people, and try to change the set times and the laws. The holy people will be delivered into his hands for 3 1/2 years, the last years of the seven-year **Tribulation Period**.

At the end of this period, his power will be taken away, and he will be cast into the **Lake of Fire**. Then the sovereignty, power, and greatness of all the kingdoms under heaven will be handed over to Jesus. His kingdom will be an everlasting kingdom, and everyone will worship and obey him. Daniel was deeply troubled by many of the visions, his face turned pale, and he told no one of his dreams.

Chapter 8: We now see a picture of God's absolute control over history, which helps us understand God's sovereignty and trust in His plans. We are now in the third year of King Belshazzar's reign, and Daniel receives his second vision. This time, he's transported in spirit to the citadel of Susa and stands beside the Ulai Canal.

In the vision, Daniel sees a **ram** with two long horns standing beside the canal. One of the horns was longer than the other, but grew later. The ram charged, and because it was so powerful, no animal could stand against it, and it became great. The ram with two high horns represents the **Medes and Persian kings**. The ram grew very powerful.

Suddenly, a **goat** with a prominent horn between its eyes came swiftly from the west and furiously charged the ram and shattered its two horns. The goat with a notable horn between his eyes symbolizes the King of Greece (**Alexander the Great**), the son of Philip, king of Macedonia. The defeated ram signifies the Greeks defeating the Medes and Persians. In six years, Alexander made himself master of the greatest part of the then-known world. He defeated **Darius Codomannus**, then emperor of Persia, in three famous victories at Granicus, Issus, and Arbela. Alexander became the absolute master of the Persian Empire. He was about twenty years old when he began his wars, and about twenty-six when he conquered Darius. He died when he was about thirty years of age, supposedly from malaria or typhoid fever. Others say that he died of excessive alcohol or that he was poisoned.

The **large horn broken off symbolizes the untimely death of Alexander the Great**. In its place, four prominent horns—**Alexander's four generals create four kingdoms**.

Out of one of them came another horn which started small but grew in power until it reached the host of the heavens. He was of fierce countenance, insolent and furious, neither fearing God nor regarding man. He will cause astounding devastation, destroy holy people, yet he will be destroyed.

A futurist view of this passage believes it is partially fulfilled by **Antiochus Epiphanies** (prefigures the *Antichrist*), who stopped sacrifices for exactly three years ending in 164 B.C. The **king symbolized by the horn refers to the Antichrist,** who in the latter days will end the sacrifices, persecute the saints, and commit the abomination of desolation, exalting himself above God.

Daniel then heard one of the holy ones ask another how long it would take for the vision to be fulfilled regarding the daily sacrifice. This rebellion causes desolation, the surrender of the sanctuary, and the trampling underfoot of the Lord's people, and the answer was **2,300** evenings and mornings. The 2,300 days represent about 6 1/3 years. It is thought that this prophecy was fulfilled before the birth of Christ, during the reign of the Seleucid king Antiochus IV (Epiphanes).

In Revelation 11–12, John mentions **1,260 days** in two prophecies concerning **another persecution of the Jews during the end times**. Daniel predicts the actions of the evil Antiochus Epiphanes, and John predicts those of an even more evil being—the Antichrist. Despite the disturbing vision, Gabriel reassures Daniel that desolation will end. The chapter ends with Daniel, exhausted and ill, and keeping the vision a secret.

Chapter 9: The timeframe is now around 539 BC, and Daniel has been in captivity for over 65 years. This chapter shows how powerful prayer can be. Despite Israel's repeated sins, God still has enduring love and is willing to forgive the nation. This chapter can be one of the most challenging, so I have broken it down verse by verse.

We are now in the first year of Darius the Mede, son of Xerxes. Daniel is reading the **Book of Jeremiah** and realizes that the <u>Jews' 70-year exile in Babylon will soon end</u>. Like a priest, Daniel has been pleading and praying for Israel, acknowledging the nation's sins against God and asking for God's mercy. Daniel was a very righteous man and identified himself with his fellow Jews and their sins.

As Daniel prays, the angel Gabriel appears and tells him that he is precious and highly esteemed and will give him a vision of Israel's future.

Gabriel said, "**Seventy sevens**" (the <u>*seventy years*</u> also called weeks) of Babylonian captivity are determined upon thy people and thy holy city, to finish the transgression, and to make an end of sins, and to make reconciliation for iniquity, and to bring in everlasting righteousness, and to seal up the vision and prophecy, and to anoint the most Holy Place (Daniel 9:24). <u>The beginning of the 70 weeks is from the going forth of the command to restore and build Jerusalem.</u>

The prophecy foretold a period of ***seventy sevens, 490 years yet to come***. The first phase of Israel's punishment was related to not allowing the land to rest every 7th year. Over 490 years, the land of Israel was shortened ***by 70 years of sabbath rest***. This led to Israel being forced to leave the land for 70 years so that the land could obtain the sabbath rest that it was due. In addition to the sin of desecrating sabbatical years, the Jews had committed other sins throughout the period occupied by these sabbatical years. For this, 70 years of exile would not suffice, and ***the full period of 490 years was needed for atonement***. These "70 Weeks" were determined or "cut out" by God and are directed primarily at the nation of Israel.

Israel must go through all 490 years;
the last 7 are the Tribulation period.

The 70 Weeks:

Verse 9:24: 70 weeks or 490 years required

Verse 9:25: The first 69 weeks or 483 years

Verse 9:26: An interval before the last week

Verse 9:27: The last week—final 7 years

"Know therefore and understand, That from the going forth of the command To restore and build Jerusalem Until Messiah the Prince, There shall be seven weeks and sixty-two weeks; The street shall be built again, and the wall, Even in troublesome times" (Daniel 9:25).

This deals directly with the beginning of the division of Daniel's prophetic clock and uses a measurement of time known as a Heptad, a group or series of seven. After **49 years**, the first part of the prophecy will be complete. Then, from that time, the decree was given to rebuild Jerusalem until the Messiah came, which was **483 years**—173,880 days based on the Jewish calendar.

As God's judgment for Judah's idolatry and rebellion, Judah was attacked by the Babylonians in 589 BC. The city of Jerusalem was destroyed. The Jews were held captive for 70 years in Babylon and, after Babylon's fall, Emperor *Cyrus the Great* of Persia decreed that the Jews would be allowed to return to Jerusalem, and some did immediately (537 B.C.).

Cyrus returned the items Nebuchadnezzar of Babylon had stolen from the temple, and *King Darius* then issued a decree in 515 B.C. to support the process. For a period, people in the surrounding lands opposed the rebuilding of Jerusalem.

In 457 B.C., *King Artaxerxes I* (Arta-xer-xes) issued a rebuilding decree and granted Nehemiah's request to help rebuild Jerusalem and the Temple (Nehemiah 6).

So, with all that said, three of the Persian kings, *Cyrus, Darius I*, and *Artaxerxes I,* contributed to a decree helping to restore Jerusalem, but it is **_Artaxerxes I's decree that fits Daniel 9:25_**. This is when the rebuilding of Jerusalem begins.

The **seven weeks (7x7=49 years)** relate to the rebuilding of Jerusalem, which took **49 years**. The **62 weeks (62x7=434 years)** relate to the coming of the Messiah, the Prince. Gabriel said the degree would be issued, seven weeks (49 years would pass), 62 weeks (434 years) would pass, and then Jesus would come. This would be AD27, the year that Jesus, the Anointed One and Messiah, was baptized and anointed by the Holy Spirit.

Jesus' purpose in riding into Jerusalem on Palm Sunday was to publicly proclaim His claim to be their Messiah and King of Israel, fulfilling Old Testament prophecy. Unfortunately, the people did not want a savior; they wanted someone to lead them in a revolt against Rome. Within just a few days, their praises would change to cries of *"Crucify Him!"* and Jesus would be abandoned.

"And after the sixty-two weeks Messiah shall be cut off, but not for Himself; And the people of the prince who is to come Shall destroy the city and the sanctuary. The end of it shall be with a flood, And till the end of the war desolations are determined" (Daniel 9:26).

The interpretation of "cut off" is thought to mean crucified. *"He did not die for himself."* His death was to atone for our sins and to purchase life for us. Jesus presented himself as the Messiah to the nation on Palm Sunday, was crucified around 32 AD, and then rose from the dead. The prophecy then states that after the Messiah is killed, *"the people of the ruler who will come and destroy the city and the sanctuary."* Within one generation of Christ's crucifixion, **Titus of Rome** destroyed Jerusalem and the Temple (70 AD).

Gabriel mentioned "a prince who is to come," and that is the Antichrist. The Romans destroyed Jerusalem and the Temple. Perhaps the Antichrist comes from the nations that made up the Old Roman Empire? The Messiah is cut off, and **the** *prophetic clock stops with one seven-year period yet to be accomplished*. This means that there is an interval between the 69th and 70th sevens.

The present Church Age is between the 69th and 70th "sevens." The Church Age will end when the **Rapture** event occurs. Israel's clock will again start ticking for the final week—the 7-year Tribulation period or *The Time of Jacob's Trouble*. At the end of the 70th week, the **Millennial Kingdom** is established.

The prophetic 70 weeks may actually be a **dual prophecy**, meaning that it may have both a short- and long-term fulfillment (Ezekiel 37). Some believe the short-term fulfillment of this prophecy occurred in 1948 when Israel became a state, and Jews from anywhere in the world could then return home. The longer-term fulfillment will be God's promise to re-gather Jews from the four corners of the world and bring them back to Israel, and Jesus will reign as king over all from Jerusalem. This is still to come after the end of the 70th week.

The Antichrist will make a pact with Israel but will break it in the middle (3 ½ years) and stop the worship of God in the Temple, replacing it with an idol or an abomination. Jesus warned of this event in Matthew 24:15. This will be a time of great tribulation. It is also stated that the Antichrist will face judgment. He only rules, "*until the end that is decreed is poured out on him.*" God will only allow evil to go so far, and the judgment the Antichrist will face has already been decided.

Chapter 10: This is the beginning of Daniel's last vision, which continues to the end of the book. The veil is lifted, and we see a spiritual world and angels as the ministers of God's government of men. The chapter also reveals a battle in the invisible angelic realm, reminding us of the spiritual battles around us. This vision takes place about two years after the vision in Chapter 9.

During the third year of Cyrus King of Persia, Daniel had a vision of a great war that troubled him. He was standing on the bank of the Tigris River, and *"someone like a son of man"* appeared before him with a belt of fine gold from Uphaz around his waist. Only Daniel saw the man.

The messenger told Daniel that the Lord had heard his prayers, and he had come to respond to them. The *prince of the Persian kingdom* had delayed him for twenty days, but *Michael*, one of the chief princes, came to help him. The messenger reveals that he will soon return to the spiritual battle with the Princes of Persia and Greece. But before doing so, he will tell Daniel what will happen to his people in the later days and what is written in the *Book of Truth*. Daniel was speechless and bowed his face toward the ground. Then the one who looked like a man touched Daniel, gave him strength, and said, *"Do not be afraid, you who are highly esteemed; be strong."*

Perhaps each empire has demonic angelic beings assigned to influence people's affairs. The apostle Paul wrote:

"Finally, be strong in the Lord and in his mighty power. Put on the full armour of God so that you can take your stand against the devil's schemes. For our struggle is not against flesh and blood, but against the rulers, against the authorities, against the powers of this dark world and against the spiritual forces of evil in the heavenly realms."

Chapter 11: contains Daniel's final vision and describes the conflicts and events between the **South and North kings**. When the Bible mentions the North and South, it is always in relation to the land of Israel. These kings are not single individuals, but rulers of the Ptolemaic Dynasty headquartered in Egypt (South) and the *Seleucid Dynasty in* **Syria (North)**. The chapter also reveals God's sovereignty and protection over those faithful to him in times of trouble.

The kings of the North and South were two dynasties that fought each other for many years. They were relevant because each generation attempted to wipe out the people of God at some point. During each war, they usually passed through Israel and did much damage.

The chapter begins during the first year of Darius the Mede. The angel states that three more kings will rise in Persia, and then a far richer and more powerful fourth king will go against the kingdom of Greece. (**King Xerxes**). **Alexander the Great** will then arise and conquer Persia, but will die at the age of 33. After his death, his empire will be broken up and given to his four powerful generals: **Lysimachus** will take Thrace (a portion of southeastern Europe) and much of Asia Minor. **Cassander** will control Macedonia and Greece. **Ptolemy** will take an area to the South of Israel, including Egypt, and Seleucus will take control of an area to the North of Israel, including Syria.

At first, Seleucus, the king of Syria, had been a subject of Ptolemy in Egypt, but over time, Ptolemy became more powerful. Princess Berenice from the South married the Seleucid king to unite the kingdoms, and a child was born from that union. But the king of the North died suddenly, and the wife and child were murdered in 246 BC. Instead of sealing an alliance, the two kingdoms went to war.

Princess Berenice's brother, *Ptolemy III* (king in Egypt), would attack and defeat the Syrian king of the North (*Seleucus II*) and would seize Syria's bounty and take it back to Egypt. It is thought that the bounty consisted of 4,000 talents of gold, 40,000 talents of silver, and 2,500 Syrian idols (Daniel 11:7–10).

Many additional battles took place, and another marriage alliance was tried. Syria tries to ally with Egypt by giving a daughter as a wife to Ptolemy. Antiochus III allies with Ptolemy V by giving him his daughter (*Cleopatra I*) as a wife, but this fails because she does not stay loyal to her father but to her husband. (This Cleopatra is not the one who later dealt with Mark Antony). It seemed that the battles and evil alliances never ended. It would be a time of great courage and great treachery among the people of God.

The **Maccabean Revolt** was a Jewish rebellion that took place because of all the terrible things being done to the Jewish people. *Antiochus III* was defeated in Greece by the Roman

General Lucius Cornelius. He was humiliated in the defeat, and needing money badly, he resorted to pillaging a Babylonian Temple and was killed by enraged local citizens. Seleucus III, the eldest son of Antiochus III, was his successor. He continued to raise taxes and was assassinated, probably by his brother Antiochus IV.

This brings us to the man known as Antiochus IV Epiphanes (Ep-pi-han-ese), who was born in 215 BC and died in 164 BC. He was the son of Antiochus III and one of the most evil and brutal kings of the North. Antiochus Epiphanes was not a legitimate heir to the throne; however, he gathered an army and seized the throne by force in 187 BC. He took his orders from Rome and was under Roman control.

He hated the people of Jerusalem, and although he took the name Epiphanes (*God manifest*), some called him "*the madman.*" He sold the office of High Priest and persecuted the Jewish people to conform to Greek culture. Antiochus set up an image of Zeus at the temple altar, demanded sacrifice to this image, and later desecrated the temple by sacrificing a pig. This was surely an abomination, bringing a desolate condition to the Temple, and no one would come to worship. In his attack on Jerusalem, Antiochus IV is said to have killed 80,000 Jews, taken 40,000 more as prisoners, and sold another 40,000 as slaves. He also robbed the temple.

Much of this chapter is seemingly on Antiochus Epiphanes, but after his time, there were other kings of the North and South. Now, attention shifts to the final world dictator in the latter days—the **Antichrist**. You might say he is sort of a "*last days Antiochus Epiphanes.*"

Even though Antiochus's career was terrible, he was not even close to the evil that the Antichrist would bring. The Antichrist will sit as God in the Temple and shall "*regard neither the God of his fathers nor the desire of women.*" Based on this, some think he will be of Jewish descent and perhaps be a homosexual. Others believe that the "*desire of women*" refers to Jesus, in that all women wanted the honor of bearing the Messiah. Many kings will attack him, and the end will be marked by a great conflict with all the world's armies gathering in the Promised Land—The Battle of Armageddon.

Chapter 12: This is the final chapter, and in it, we see a period of unmatched distress, the promise of resurrection and judgment, and the sealing of these prophecies until the end time. The people of God will be comforted to know that the archangel **Michael** is on their side, and they have the promise of deliverance. Michael is often associated with spiritual battle and is called Satan's true opposite. In addition to his role as a spiritual warrior, God appointed Michael as a spiritual guardian over Israel. This time of persecution for Israel and the world is called the Tribulation.

> Jesus said, *"For then there will be great tribulation, such as has not been since the beginning of the world until this time, no, nor ever shall be"* (Matthew 24:21).

Satan will direct his fury against the Jewish people during this time, but God promises to preserve them.

> God promised Abraham, *"And I will establish My covenant between Me and you and your descendants after you in their generations, for an everlasting covenant, to be God to you and your descendants after you"* (Genesis 17:7).

Romans 11:25-27 states that Israel will eventually be known as a people who trust in Jesus as their Messiah and truly turn to the Lord. However, not every person of Jewish heritage will be saved, only those found written in the Book of Life.

The Bible teaches two resurrections, one for the saved and one for the damned (John 5:29; Revelation 20:4-6; and Revelation 11:15). Multitudes who sleep in the dust of the earth will awake, some to everlasting life, others to shame and everlasting contempt (Hell). Despite all the difficulties coming upon Israel, God's promises will apply to all who believe in

Jesus. There will be 144,000 evangelists from Israel's tribes during the Tribulation.

Daniel is then told to roll up and seal the scroll's words until the end. Then Daniel looked, and there stood two others, one on this bank of the river and one on the opposite bank. One of them said to the man clothed in linen, who was above the river's waters, *"How long will it be before these astonishing things are fulfilled?"*

A man clothed in linen who was above the waters of the river, lifted both his hands and Daniel heard him swear by him who lives forever, saying, *"It will be for a **time, times and half a time (3 ½ years)**. When the power of the holy people has been finally broken,* the period that saints are given into the Antichrist's hands, *all these things will be completed."* This period was described as the time between the breaking of Antichrist's covenant with Israel, the erection of the abomination of desolation, and the establishment of Jesus' kingdom.

The Tribulation is a time when God preserves a remnant of Israel in the wilderness. The last 3 ½ years are known as the Great Tribulation, and at the end, Jesus returns. The Antichrist's authority to rule, persecute, and blaspheme will end.

Daniel didn't understand it all, even though he heard it firsthand. These things will not be revealed until the end, and until then, these prophecies are closed and sealed.

"From the time that the daily sacrifice is abolished and the abomination that causes desolation is set up, there will be 1,290 days. Blessed is the one who waits for and reaches the end of the 1,335 days."

God made it clear that He would purify and preserve His people and set a limit of days for the time of trouble. The messenger stated that from the time the daily sacrifice is taken away, and the abomination of desolation is set up, there shall be ***1,290*** days. It is difficult to say what the relationship is between the three and a half years mentioned in many places (**1260 days**), and the **1290 days** mentioned here. The *Abomination of Desolation* will remain for an extra 30 days.

This may be one of those things we are not meant to know. Some think it will be related to the time needed to rid the earth of the Antichrist's impact, or the time to gather the Elect and assemble them in Israel. Others think it will be a period of grace before judgment.

And now we have **1335 days** mentioned (**1335 minus 1290 = 45 days**). Again, we are not told the reason for this number; however, something happens at the end of the 45 days that will make some people happy.

Some think that this will be when Jesus judges the nations. Some will be blessed by entering the Millennial Kingdom, while others will be cursed and enter the Lake of Fire (Matthew 25:31–46).

Perhaps Jesus's government is officially installed at the end of the **1260 days**, and the nations are judged at the end of the **1335 days**.

Daniel was told that the words were to be closed and sealed until the end. This should make us think differently about Bible prophecy because God's plans always come true. Daniel was not to spend all his time and energy speculating and worrying about things he couldn't understand. Instead, he should simply obey the word to go his way until the end—something we must all do.

We know the Book of Daniel is complete because no other visions were recorded. We also know that God may not have intended us to understand everything in the Book of Daniel— He just wants us to trust Him in all He does.

Daniel lived for about 80–plus years, during which time his entire life was built around trusting God. What a great story.

Other Interesting Items to Consider:

- The books of Daniel and Revelation are often studied together because their prophecies concerning the end times dovetail with each other nicely.

- People today think in units of tens (**Decades**). Daniel's people thought in units of sevens (**Heptad's**) and also **Septets**—a designation of a prophetic period of time measured by the number seven.

- The *chronological order* of the Book of Daniel is chapters 1-4, 7-8, 5-6, and 9-12. Notice that chapters 5-6 and chapters 7-8 are flip-flopped with each other.

- In calculating years from **B.C. to A.D.**, one must always be omitted. From B.C. 1 to A.D. 1 is one year, not two years. B.C. 1 is calculated as B.C. 0 by astronomers; therefore, what is commonly referred to as 445 B.C. is referred to as 444 B.C. by astronomers.

- During the latter half of the 6th century BC, both the ancient Hebrews and Babylonians used a 360-day **year** (Advent Calendar).

In summary, perhaps this is a suggested timeline from the Rapture until the New Heavens and New Earth:

- Sometime after the Rapture of the church, the Antichrist enters into a treaty with Israel. This begins the seven-year Tribulation.

- At the midpoint of the Tribulation (1,260 days later), the Antichrist breaks the treaty, desecrates the temple, and begins to persecute the Jews.

- At the end of the Great Tribulation (<u>1,260 days after the desecration of the temple</u>), Jesus Christ returns to earth and defeats the forces of the Antichrist (Battle of Armageddon).

- During the next 30 days, leading up to 1,290 days after the desecration of the temple, perhaps Israel will be rebuilt, and the earth will be restored.

- During the next 45 days, leading up to 1,335 days after the desecration of the temple, the nations are possibly judged for their treatment of Israel.

- The dispensation of the Millennium begins, and it will last for 1,000 years (Revelation 20:3, 5-6).

70 "Sevens" or "Weeks": "seventy sevens" (or seventy weeks), which is interpreted as **490 years**.

1,260 days: 42 months, or **3 ½ years**.

Time, Times and half a time: 3 ½ years

1290 Days: This period is described as a time when the "daily sacrifice" will be removed, and the "Abomination of Desolation" will be set up.

45 Days (1335 - 1290 = 45): An additional 45 days are added to the 1290 days, bringing the total to 1335 days. This may be when the Judgment of the Nations occurs (Matthew 25:31-46).

Judgment of the Nations: The 1335 days, and the 45 days leading up to it, are often associated with the judgment of the nations for their treatment of Israel (Sheep/Goats).

1335 Days: This period is described as a time of "blessedness" for those who wait and arrive at this time and is associated with the judgment of the nations.

Starting Point: The 70 weeks begin "from the going forth of the command to restore and build Jerusalem."

Divided Time Periods: The 70 weeks are further divided into three periods: **Seven Weeks (49 years)**. During this time, Jerusalem was to be rebuilt. **Sixty-two Weeks (434 years): After the 49 years, the Messiah would come. One Week (7 years):** This period includes the Messiah's death and the destruction of Jerusalem.

The **70 weeks** are often seen as a **prophetic "clock"** that provides a timeframe for the events surrounding the Messiah's coming.

Timeline: *Daniel was probably born about 620–618 BC and died after Cyrus conquered Babylon in 538 BC, making him 80+ years old.

598 BC: King Jehoiakim of Judah reigned

605 BC: Nebuchadnezzar's reign – Daniel in Babylon

603 BC: Nebuchadnezzar's 1st dream – Statue

585 BC: Three friends of Daniel thrown into the Furnace

562 BC: Nebuchadnezzar's 2nd dream about the Tree

544 BC: Vision of 4 Beasts – Vision of Ram – Goat

539 BC: Handwriting on Wall – Daniel in the Lion's Den

537 BC: Vision of Anointed One – End Times

430 BC: Jews return to Israel

333 BC: Israel falls to Greece

323 BC: Israel falls to Egypt

171 BC: Antiochus Epiphanes Desecrates Temple

165 BC: Jews recapture Jerusalem

63 BC: Rome takes control.

47 BC: Caesar appoints Antipater

*Jesus was born around 6 to 4 BC. Luke 3:23 shows us that Jesus was about thirty when he started his ministry and was in it for three years. Jesus would have been about 32 or 33 years old at the time of His crucifixion.

*The time between the Old Testament's last writings and Christ's appearance is known as the "***Intertestamental Period***." It lasted from the prophet Malachi's time (about 400 BC) to the preaching of John the Baptist (about AD 25). Because there was no prophetic word from God during this period, some refer to it as the "***400 silent years***."

Kings During Daniel's Time:

King Jehoiakim: Named Eliakim at birth, was one of the last kings of Judah before the Babylonian captivity and reigned eleven years. Jehoiakim was a son of King Josiah, who had returned Judah to the Lord by tearing down idol shrines and restoring obedience to God's Law. After Josiah's death, his son Jehoahaz was chosen king, but he did evil in the sight of the Lord. Joahaz only reigned three months before he was taken into captivity by the king of Egypt, who replaced him with his brother Eliakim (2 Kings 23:26; 2 Chronicles 36:5).

The Egyptian king renamed the 25-year-old Eliakim "Jehoiakim." But Jehoiakim also did evil in the Lord's sight, and God sent invading armies to capture and enslave the nation. Jehoiakim was taken captive by King Nebuchadnezzar, who put him in chains and sent him to Babylon. At this time, Daniel and his three friends were also taken to Babylon.

King Nebuchadnezzar: Also spelled Nebuchadrezzar, was king of Babylonia from approximately 605 BC until approximately 562 BC. Thought to be the greatest king of the Babylonian Empire and is credited with constructing the Hanging Gardens of Babylon. Nebuchadnezzar is mentioned by name around 90 times in the Bible. Nebuchadnezzar was a brutal and ambitious king. Judah had become rebellious in 597 BC during the reign of Jehoiachin and then again in 588 BC during the reign of Zedekiah. Nebuchadnezzar and his general, *Nebuzaradan*, invaded Judah in 586 BC, destroyed the Temple and most of Jerusalem, and deported many residents to Babylon. Nebuchadnezzar served as God's instrument of judgment on Judah for its idolatry, unfaithfulness, and disobedience (Jeremiah 25:9). History records Nebuchadnezzar as a follower of the Babylonian gods Nabu and Marduk. Still, many believe that Nebuchadnezzar eventually submitted himself to the one true God. If you think Nebuchadnezzar was not bad, read Jeremiah 52:4-13.

King Belshazzar of Babylon: He was the last king of ancient Babylon and reigned briefly during the life of Daniel the prophet. His name, meaning *"Bel protect the king,"* is a prayer to a Babylonian god, and he was an evil ruler. Belshazzar was Nebuchadnezzar's grandson through his daughter Nitocris. Belshazzar calls Nebuchadnezzar his "father" (Daniel 5:13), but this is a generic use of the word father, meaning "ancestor."

Belshazzar is best remembered for filling the gold and silver cups and vessels taken by Nebuchadnezzar from the Jewish temple with wine and then praising their false gods. A human hand appeared and wrote words that told of Belshazzar's kingdom being divided between the Medes and Persians. That very night, Belshazzar was slain, and Darius the Mede took over the kingdom.

King Nabonidus of Babylon: He reigned from 556 until 539 BC, when Babylon fell to Cyrus, king of Persia. After a popular uprising led by the priests of Marduk, chief god of the city, Nabonidus, who favored the moon god Sin, made his son Belshazzar co-ruler, and spent much of his reign in Arabia. Returning to Babylon in 539 BC, he was captured by Cyrus' army. Belshazzar was his son, who had been left in charge for 11 years while Nabonidus was holed up in Tayma, a distant oasis in the Arabian Desert. Remember that Daniel was offered to be the "third one" in the kingdom if he could tell the meaning of the writing on the wall. Belshazzar was the second king of the kingdom.

King Darius the Mede: He ruled for only two years (539-536 BC) and is best known as the ruler who promoted Daniel to a high position in the kingdom and then cast him into the lions' den, much against his better judgment. The word Darius means "lord." Daniel 6:28 refers to "the reign of Darius and the reign of Cyrus the Persian," showing that Darius and Cyrus ruled concurrently. This has caused Bible scholars to posit that Darius was appointed viceroy over Babylon by his nephew, King Cyrus. There are other references to rulers named Darius in the Bible.

Cyrus the Great: Also known as Cyrus II or Cyrus the Persian, **he reigned over Persia between 539 and** 530 BC. Jewish history shows that under his rule, Jews were first allowed to return to Israel after 70 years of captivity. King Cyrus was instrumental in helping the Jews rebuild the Temple in Jerusalem under the direction of Zerubbabel and Joshua the high priest.

The Book of Ezekiel

The prophet Ezekiel was born around 622 BC and grew up in Jerusalem, where he trained as a priest. Ezekiel, also spelled Ezechiel in Hebrew, means *"God is strong"* or *"God strengthens."* He came from Levi, a tribe consecrated explicitly for the priesthood, and his father was Buzi (bu–z), also a priest. This  upbringing equipped Ezekiel with a deep understanding of the rituals and customs of the Jewish faith.

The Book of Ezekiel has 48 chapters and can be put into four divisions: (1) The Commission of Ezekiel, (2) Judgment of Judah, (3) Judgment on the Nations, and (4) Restoration of Israel. While in Babylon, Ezekiel became a prophet of God. This book announces the destruction of Judah's capital city,

Jerusalem, but Ezekiel's prophecies speak of hope for the future, and he wants to help the people learn from their failures. His prophetic ministry was trying to bring the people to immediate repentance.

Ezekiel dates his first divine encounter to "the 30th year," which appears to refer to his age of 30, the year he would have been eligible for priesthood. It is "the fifth of the month in the fifth year of King Jehoiachin (j–ho–i–hin) of Judah's exile." This would be 593 BC, since Jehoiachin was taken from Jerusalem to Babylon in 597 BC. The last recorded prophecy of Ezekiel dates to 571 BC, sixteen years after the destruction of Jerusalem in 587 BC. Ezekiel's prophecies occurred over approximately 22 years. There are six dated visions and 13 prophecies mentioned in the book. As a prominent prophet of the time, he has been called "the father of Judaism" and the "prophet of visions." While the Bible does not provide an exact date for Ezekiel's death, it is believed to have occurred around 571 BC.

A bit of history about the area: Israel is referred to as 12 tribes forming one nation; however, after King Solomon's death, the nation split into two parts. The **10 northern tribes** (Reuben, Simeon, Manasseh, Issachar, Zebulun, Ephraim, Dan, Asher, Naphtali, and Gad) continued to be called *Israel* (or Samaria), and the **southern tribes** (Judah, Benjamin, and part of Levi) were named *Judah*. The northern tribes were continually disobedient and were taken by Assyria into slavery. The southern tribes were also very sinful and were conquered by Babylon and deported several times.

The first siege of Jerusalem was by Babylon (Chaldeans), and the exile was in ***605 BC.*** Ezekiel was about 18 when 15-year-old **Daniel** and his three friends were captured by **Nebuchadnezzar** and taken to Babylon. Ezekiel was left behind in Jerusalem.

Babylon's second siege of Jerusalem occurred in 597 BC. Ezekiel was about 26 years old and was among the second group of 10,000 captives, which included King Jehoiachin. The

Babylonian Exile, also known as the Babylonian Captivity, was a significant event in ancient Israel's history.

The third Siege of Jerusalem by Babylon began in 588 BC and ended in **586 BC.** Jerusalem was captured, and the Temple and city walls were destroyed. Ezekiel would see visions of a future temple and a new Jerusalem.

An Overview of the Book of Ezekiel

Ezekiel's 1st vision was on the banks of the Kebar River (Chebar), where in spirit he sees the likeness of the Glory of God and describes four living creatures and whirling wheels.

> *"I looked, and I saw a windstorm coming out of the north— an immense cloud with flashing lightning and surrounded by brilliant light. The center of the fire looked like glowing metal, and in the fire was what looked like four living creatures"* (Ezekiel 1:4–28).

Four living creatures appear from the whirlwind. There is a firmament above the creatures, and above the firmament Ezekiel sees, *"the likeness of a throne,"* and seated on it, *"**the likeness of a man**."* The four living creatures have human form, but each has four faces—that of a man, a lion, an ox, and an eagle, and each has four wings. These creatures are later revealed as cherubim.

A **wheel** on the earth is alongside each creature, and the wheels appear like a wheel intersecting another wheel. They gleam like chrysolite and have eyes covering them all around. The many eyes represent God as all-wise, all-knowing, all-seeing, and they moved straight forward without turning, symbolizing God's absolute righteousness and truth from which he never turns aside.

The **throne** above the firmament symbolizes God's heavenly throne and sovereignty. This figure is bright, like a rainbow in the clouds on a rainy day. It is a likeness of the **Glory of the God of Israel**.

Interestingly, the apostle John was likewise shown a glimpse of the heavenly realm and Glory of God before he received great prophecies of the future (Revelation 1,4). God required Ezekiel to eat a scroll, which may have included the written words God spoke to him (Ezekiel 3:1-10). This act signifies that Ezekiel must fully absorb and embody the message of God, making it a part of himself, before presenting the message to the people of Israel. The scroll represents divine wisdom and prophecy. As Ezekiel consumes the scroll, it tastes as sweet as honey, symbolizing the sweetness of God's words even amid the bitterness of judgment.

God then commissioned Ezekiel as a "**Watchman for the House of Israel**." Despite Israel's rebelliousness, God is giving them another chance. John is also instructed to eat a scroll, signifying the acceptance and proclamation of God's message (Revelation 10).

> "He said: 'son of man, I am sending you to the Israelites, to a rebellious nation that has rebelled against me; they and their fathers have been in revolt against me to this very day. The people to whom I am sending you are obstinate and stubborn. Say to them, "This is what the Sovereign LORD says. And whether they listen or fail to listen—for they are a rebellious house—they will know that a prophet has been among them" (Ezekiel 2:3-6). Ezekiel delivered this message to the people.

Ezekiel was overwhelmed with grief by his people's sins and miseries, and he hoped that God's words through him as a Watchman for the House of Israel would cause them to repent. Ezekiel is instructed to go to the Plains, where he experiences God's glory again.

God then commands Ezekiel to sketch a picture of Jerusalem on a clay tablet. This act symbolizes the impending Babylonian siege and serves as a visual warning to the people about the judgment that will come upon them. God commands Ezekiel to lie on his left side for **390 days** and on his right side for **40 days**. The 390 days represent the number of years the people of Israel had sinned, and the 40 days represent the number of years that the people of Judah had sinned. Idolatry and sin have spread throughout the land, and up until now, God has been very patient dealing with the sins.

Chapter 5 is the **Prophecy of the Thirds**. Using his cut hair, Ezekiel depicts how Jerusalem was to be punished for its sins. One-third of Israel will perish by fire, one-third will perish by military conquest, and the surviving third will be forced into servitude in foreign lands. Ezekiel is instructed to bind a few hairs on the edge of his garment, indicating that a small remnant of people will be preserved. This prophecy is a warning of what could befall the nations of Israel now and possibly in the future. This future time of extreme trouble will be known as *"Jacob's Trouble"* (Jeremiah 30:4-7).

Ezekiel now prophesied against much of Israel because the Israelites had built many places for idol worship. God promises to bring down these altars, smash their idols, and lay the bodies of the Israelites among their broken idols. His wrath will make them understand that He is the Lord. But even in His wrath, God promises that a remnant of the Israelites will survive. This presents a grim picture of the inescapable consequences of sin and unfaithfulness to God.

The prophet is then transported in a vision to Jerusalem, where a fiery being representing the Glory of God shows him the corruption and idolatry of His people (and elders) within the sacred Temple. The Temple's intended purity and the abominations taking place set the stage for God's judgment.

Ezekiel hears God's voice summoning six executioners, including a man dressed in linen with a writer's inkhorn. God commands the man to mark the foreheads of those in Jerusalem who have not practiced these abominations. They will be protected from the judgments. The six men with deadly weapons are then to slaughter all of those who do not bear the protective mark (vs. 9).

Ezekiel then sees God's glory depart from the Temple threshold, move above the cherubim, and stand at the entrance of the east gate of the Lord's house. This marks a heart-wrenching moment of divine abandonment due to Jerusalem's sinful ways. **The departure of God's Glory from the Temple illustrates the consequences of disobedience.**

Ezekiel is then told to address the people's misguided belief that the prophecies of doom are for the distant future. Ezekiel performs symbolic acts representing the forthcoming exile of the inhabitants of Jerusalem, including its prince. The prince refers to the leader or ruler in Jerusalem at the time, and here it is probably **King Zedekiah** (zed-e-kia). This prince will try to escape the city but will be captured and brought to Babylon. God once again refers to the Israelites as a rebellious house, highlighting their persistent disobedience and refusal to heed His warnings. The Israelites are warned that they will be scattered among the nations.

God now issues a warning to **false prophets**. *"Woe to the foolish prophets who follow their own spirit and have seen nothing!"* God condemns those who speak from their imagination rather than His truth.

Elders from the Israelite community come to Ezekiel seeking wisdom, but God reveals to Ezekiel that these elders harbor idols in their hearts. The Israelites are told to repent and turn away from their idols before God's impending judgment in Jerusalem is made.

A metaphor about ***vine wood*** is used to describe the people of Jerusalem. Unlike other trees, vine wood is not useful for construction or crafting; its primary purpose is to bear fruit. This imagery highlights the expectation that Israel, as God's chosen people, should produce spiritual fruit. It emphasizes the necessity of fruitfulness and the consequences of not living according to God's purpose. The vine represents the land of Jerusalem. Just as a vine is destined for fire due to its lack of usefulness, so is Jerusalem destined for fire and destruction because of its disobedience.

Jerusalem is described as having a humble origin. God recalls how He found Jerusalem, also called Israel, cared for it, and brought it to glory. But despite being divinely blessed,

Jerusalem betrayed God's trust by engaging in spiritual adultery, worshipping false idols, and forming alliances with foreign nations. Jerusalem's sins are like those of the cities of Sodom and Samaria. But even through all this, God reassures the people that He will remember His covenant and promises to restore Jerusalem.

A parable involving **eagles and vines** (symbolizing political alliances and betrayals) is now presented. The first eagle, representing the king of Babylon (Nebuchadnezzar), breaks off the top of a cedar, symbolizing the Davidic monarchy, and carries it to a city of merchants (Babylon). The second eagle (Egypt) with a vine (Israel) bends its roots toward this eagle, seeking support and breaking its covenant with Babylon. This illustrates Israel's failed attempt to ally with Egypt.

This speaks of God's sovereignty, the consequence of disloyalty, and the divine promise of restoration. Jerusalem is symbolized as a useless vine. God promises to take a tender sprig from the top of a cedar and plant it on a high mountain in Israel. This represents the future restoration and establishment of a righteous kingdom under the Messiah, and the ultimate blessing to all nations.

God states that regardless of your past, it is never too late to turn back and seek God's forgiveness. No burden of sin is too heavy for repentance to lift. God declares that each life is precious to Him, but each person is responsible for their own sin. This verse underscores the principle that a person is not responsible for the sins of their parents or children. God's ways are just, and human ways are usually unjust. This challenges us to trust in God's perfect justice and mercy.

A metaphor of a **lioness and her cubs** describes Israel's royal lineage and downfall (Ezekiel 19). The lioness's cubs are captured and taken into captivity (Egypt and Babylon), symbolizing the downfall of Israel's leaders and the nation's later suffering. The lioness embodies a fierce and formidable presence, used to describe nations or leaders with significant power. A vine growing by the waters thrives but is eventually uprooted, symbolizing Israel's destruction.

The elders of Israel come to Ezekiel seeking guidance from God, and Ezekiel recounts Israel's history, from their time in Egypt to their entry into the Promised Land. God's faithfulness is evident as He guides, protects, and provides for them.

However, the recurring theme here is Israel's disobedience, idolatry, and rebellion against God's commands. Ezekiel is commanded to prophesy against the nations, foretelling their doom with a sword, symbolizing the intense destruction to come.

Ezekiel foretells God's judgment upon the Ammonites, a neighboring nation of Israel. God uses the king of Babylon as an instrument of His judgment, showing that even pagan nations are under His sovereign control.

Focus shifts to **Zedekiah**, the last King of Judah. He will be dethroned, symbolizing the end of the Judean monarchy until the coming of the *"one to whom it rightfully belongs."* This refers to God's promise to David that his throne would endure forever, ultimately fulfilled by **Jesus Christ**. This verse reveals God's sovereignty over leadership and history.

God now outlines the various sins of Jerusalem, including sabbath-breaking, bloodshed, idolatry, and social injustice. The city is described as a city of bloodshed (Ezekiel 22:2). There is corruption among the leaders, including prophets, priests, and princes. They are accused of exploiting the people and not upholding justice, which leads to widespread moral decay. God will purify the city through judgment and restore righteousness. God desires to find someone to stand in the gap for the land, but none is found. This verse emphasizes the importance of righteous individuals who can intercede on behalf of others to prevent destruction.

God gives Ezekiel a message in the form of a story about two sisters. **Oholah** (o-ho-la) represents **Samaria**, the capital city of the northern kingdom of Israel, and **Oholibah** (o-ho-la-ba) represents **Jerusalem**, the capital of the southern kingdom of Judah. These symbolic names represent unfaithful people who have turned to idolatry and paganism. Because of their intense idolatry and lack of faith in God, Ezekiel pronounces judgments against both kingdoms. Here, we see a stern reminder that kingdoms will face the consequences of their sins and that God's laws cannot be violated without severe penalty.

God conveys the impending judgment in Jerusalem through two symbolic events: **a boiling pot** and **the death of Ezekiel's wife**. The boiling pot represents Jerusalem, which is now filled with corruption and violence. The choice of pieces of meat symbolizes the people of Jerusalem, and the fire signifies God's wrath. The parable narrates the destruction of Jerusalem by King Nebuchadnezzar. Ezekiel's sorrow at this moment is compounded by the death of his wife, an event that God forbade him to weep over. "The word of the LORD came to me: 'Son of man, with one blow I am about to take away from you the delight of your eyes" (Ezekiel 24).

God used the death of Ezekiel's wife as a sign to the people of Judah. Just as the prophet lost his wife, the people of Judah would lose their temple. And, just as Ezekiel was instructed not to show outward signs of mourning, the Jews would be overwhelmed to the point of silence by the sorrow they felt. The death of Ezekiel's wife and his response are a prophetic sign to the Israelites, showing that they, too, will experience loss and devastation of their sacred temple without the opportunity to mourn.

God is not only the God of Israel but also holds all nations accountable for their actions. Judgment is against the *Ammonites* for their gloating over Israel's misfortune, *Moab* for equating God's chosen people to other sinful nations, *Edom* for ruthlessly attacking Israel, and *Philistia*, which wanted revenge and wronged Israel gravely. Their aggressive acts will be met with divine retribution, signifying the severe consequences of perpetuating hate.

We are now foretold the future of the ***city of Tyre*** (ti-r), a significant seaport in ancient Phoenicia. The city was known for building its wealth by exploiting its neighbors and received some of the strongest prophetic condemnations in the Bible.

God speaks against the **prince of Tyre**, who is charged with pride, extreme arrogance, and claiming to be a god.

> *"Son of man, say to the prince of Tyre, This is what the Lord GOD says: Your heart is proud, and you have said, "I am a god; I sit in the seat of gods in the heart of the sea. Yet you are a man and not a god, though you have regarded your heart as that of a god"* (Ezekiel 28:2).

But a bit later, God addresses the **King of Tyre**. This figure is often interpreted as a symbolic representation of Satan due to the description of his former perfection and later fall. The passage describes his beauty, wisdom, and eventual corruption.

> *"Son of man, take up a lament for the king of Tyre and tell him that this is what the Lord GOD says: 'You were the seal of perfection, full of wisdom and perfect in beauty. You were in Eden, the garden of God; every kind of precious stone adorned you..."* (28:12-13).

Some have proposed that Satan possessed the King of Tyre. Perhaps the text emphasizes God's sovereignty and authority over human rulers and all spiritual beings.

God's attention now turns to **Sidon** (si-dun) where He promises to send a plague and execute judgments within it. God promises that Israel will no longer suffer from the scorn of neighboring nations. He will gather the Israelites from their diaspora, provide them a peaceful dwelling in their own land, and reveal Himself as their God.

A prophetic message is now given about Egypt's fate and its ruler, Pharaoh, who is described as a "monster of the seas" destined for disgrace. God will humiliate and bring down Egypt, and Egypt will be given to Nebuchadnezzar. God promises that He will eventually restore Egypt, but not to its former glory. Israel will never again be tempted to rely on it and forget the Lord.

Ezekiel describes a day of doom for Egypt and all her allies; Cush, Put, Lud, Arabia, Libya, and the people of the covenant land. This prophecy foretells the sword falling upon them, again symbolizing God's wrath and judgment.

In Lebanon, Assyria is described as a magnificent cedar, symbolizing its glory and power. But it falls due to its pride and arrogance. God underscores the catastrophic consequences of other nations' arrogance and defiance of His sovereignty.

A lamentation for Pharaoh and Egypt is found in Ezekiel 32 and offers a view of God's judgment on nations that place their trust in their might and oppress the people of God. Egypt will fall just like other nations that have opposed God and join the others in the *"realm of the dead."*

We are reminded that Ezekiel is the "Watchman for the House of Israel," and his role is to hear the word from God's mouth and give the people warning from Him (Ezekiel 33:7). He is to alert others of the consequences of living in sin. If a watchman sees danger approaching and does not warn the people, their blood is on his hands. But if he alerts the people, he has fulfilled his duty, even if they don't heed the warning.

A fugitive arrives from Jerusalem to inform Ezekiel that the city has fallen. This event fulfills the prophecy and marks a turning point in Ezekiel's ministry. God told Ezekiel that the people treated his messages as entertainment rather than divine warnings. However, when the prophecies occur, they will know that a prophet has been among them.

Ezekiel addresses the failures of Israel's leaders, referred to as shepherds, who neglected and oppressed their people (*the flock*). God rebukes these leaders for their selfishness and failure to protect and guide the nation. **Yahweh** is presented as the good shepherd and will take care of His people and hold the wicked leaders accountable for their actions.

Now the Prophet Ezekiel announces God's judgment on **Mount Seir** (se-r), home of the *Edomites*, who had harbored age-old hostility against Israel. God accuses the Edomites of harboring a perpetual hatred against the people of Israel and for shedding their blood. This emphasizes God's wrath on those who harm his chosen people.

God now gives a message of hope and restoration for Israel. He promises that the land will once again be fruitful and increase in population after enduring scorn from surrounding nations. Israel will be restored, not for their sake, but to uphold His holy name. God promises to cleanse them from all their impurities and give them a new heart and spirit. Israel will be restored to her land in blessing under the leadership of a descendant of David—a reference to the future under **Jesus Christ the Messiah**. Israel and Judah will once again be restored to unity. This prophecy about the future Messiah was fulfilled when Jesus was born in Bethlehem more than 500 years later.

The unification and restoration of Israel seemed impossible, so now God gives Ezekiel another vision. In this vision, Ezekiel saw a **valley full of dry bones**. God instructed him to speak to the bones and tell them that God would make breath enter them, and they would come to life. Ezekiel obeyed, the bones came together, flesh developed, skin covered the flesh, breath entered the bodies, and they stood up in a vast army. This vision symbolized the whole house of Israel and God's plan for Israel's future national restoration. Israel's new life depended on God's power, and God would restore them physically and spiritually during the Millennial reign of Christ on earth.

We now come to the vision of the "latter days" (Ezekiel 38). Here we see a detailed prophecy against **Gog**, the leader of the land of **Magog**, the chief prince of Meshech and Tubal. A coalition of nations will join forces with Gog for a battle against Israel. At the time of the invasion, Israel is described as living securely and at peace, without walls or bars. Gog's motive is to plunder and loot, targeting land that has recovered from war and is prosperous.

Through Ezekiel, God speaks directly to Gog, saying He will bring Gog against Israel so that the nations will know He is sovereign. God then causes plagues, bloodshed, and other calamities against Gog's forces. Gog and his army are defeated, and the Israelites burn the enemy's weapons and cleanse the land by burying the corpses in the Valley of the Travelers. A symbolic feast for the birds and beasts takes place, and God promises the restoration of Israel and a renewed relationship with God. The ultimate purpose of these events is to reveal God's glory and sovereignty to the nations.

Although the terms Gog and Magog appear in proximity in both the Book of Ezekiel and the Book of Revelation (20:8), comparing these passages seems to indicate that two different historical events occur. The events preceding and following the battles are quite different. In Ezekiel's prophecy, the battle of Gog and Magog is used by God to draw Israel to Himself. In Revelation, the battle of Gog and Magog comes as Jesus returns before the 1000-year Millennium. Therefore, placing Ezekiel's battle in or before the Tribulation might be best.

Despite their transgressions, God hasn't forsaken His people. Ezekiel now vividly represents God's promise for Israel's future. Even though Ezekiel is still in Babylon, he is taken by spirit and sees a preview of the land Christ will reign over during and after the Millennium. He views the land not as it is in his day but as it will be after Christ returns.

Led by an angelic guide, the prophet Ezekiel records the specific dimensions and structures of a divinely designed **Temple**. God also provides specific instructions about the sacred land and how each temple room would be constructed. He emphasizes the importance of holiness, reverence, and obedience to God's commands. God also provides detailed instructions concerning worship and priesthood. He instructs explicitly the Levites and the Zadokite priests in their roles and responsibilities in this new order. God's meticulous plan reminds us of the reverence we owe to sacred places.

Ezekiel witnesses the ***return of God's Glory*** as He enters the Temple through the East Gate. The divine presence fills the Temple, and God affirms that the Temple is His throne, dwelling place, and place where He will live among His people. This points to a theme that resonates throughout Scripture:

God desires to dwell among His people. God's worship should not be taken lightly, and those who lead the people in worship should do so with the utmost reverence, sincerity, and devotion.

Ezekiel is now shown a stream of water flowing from the Temple, growing deeper as it expands outward. The increasing depth of the river illustrates the gradual growth of spiritual transformation and God's blessings. Wherever the river flows, it brings life. Trees growing alongside the river bear fruit all year round, and their leaves provide healing. This symbolizes the restoration and abundance that God brings to His people.

We are now presented with an intricate divine plan for allocating the Promised Land among the Twelve Tribes of Israel. The seven tribes of the North are Dan, Asher, Naphtali, Manasseh, Ephraim, Reuben, and Judah. Southern Tribes include Benjamin, Simeon, Issachar, Zebulun, and Gad.

The holy city layout includes the twelve gates named after the twelve tribes of Israel. The city is given a new name: "The Lord is There," signifying God's perpetual presence among His people (Ezekiel 48:35).

Ezekiel was utterly devoted to God's Word and used various methods to convey God's message to His people. He is one of the Major Prophets and received messages and visions from God during extreme upheaval. The book of Ezekiel is a prophetic work that provides a blend of judgment and hope for the people. Ezekiel is a watchman, delivering messages of impending judgment due to Israel's unfaithfulness. However, at the same time, he also unfolds visions that highlight the magnitude of God's mercy and plan for restoration.

The book records Ezekiel's ministry and service as a religious leader to the exiles from Judah who were taken to Babylon by the foreign power of Babylon. We get to look at the nation of Israel and the future of the coming Messiah, the Temple, and the Kingdom of God in the end times.

The Book of Ezekiel calls us to have a living encounter with the God of Abraham, Moses, and the prophets. It challenges us to experience a life-changing vision of God's power, knowledge, and holiness. It also wants us to experience a living relationship with God's son, Jesus Christ.

Temple History and Future

The dictionary states that a **Sanctuary** serves as a place of refuge and safety. It is sometimes referred to as a **Tabernacle**, meaning a fixed or movable habitation often used as a gathering place for prayer. The word **Temple** is derived from the Latin term *"templum"* meaning "big house." The word is usually associated with a building reserved for spiritual rituals and activities such as prayer and sacrifice. In this study, we will look at the history of these gathering places used to worship God, with particular emphasis on a third yet to be built temple mentioned in the Book of Ezekiel, and the end-of-times Millennial Temple.

Sanctuary: God had directed the Israelites to build Him a sanctuary that could easily be moved as they journeyed through the wilderness (Exodus 25:8). Since these people were traveling tribes, a tent served as a place to perform rituals and worship God. The sanctuary was supernaturally marked at its inception as God's appointed place (Exodus 33:9). The centerpiece of the sanctuary was the *Holy of Holies*, where they placed *the Ark of the Covenant* that held the manifest presence of God behind a thick veil.

King David wanted to build a permanent and great temple for God, but was forbidden. God said, "You will not build a house for my name, for you are a man of battles and have shed blood" (1 Chronicles 28:3). Instead, God promised David that his throne would be established forever, and that David's son **Solomon** would build the Temple for God.

The Altar: King David had bought a threshing floor site and supplies from **Araunah the Jebusite** to make sacrifices to the Lord. The threshing floor was a large, open, elevated area to ease threshing (*the process of separating grain from corn or other crops*) and winnowing (*blowing a current of air through grain to remove the chaff*). The **prophet Gad**, communicating

God's will, told David to build an altar to the Lord on Araunah's threshing floor.

An altar is a table or platform for the presentation of religious offerings, for sacrifices, or other ritualistic purposes. David told Araunah what he intended to do and offered to buy the threshing floor, but Araunah offered to donate the site and oxen for the offering and the threshing sledges for wood.

David refused his offer and explained, *"No, I insist on paying you for it. I will not sacrifice to the Lord my God burnt offerings that cost me nothing."* David said that a sacrifice that costs nothing is not a real sacrifice. David paid Araunah six hundred shekels of gold for the site.

After sacrificing to God from this location and being answered there by God, David said, *"This is the house of the LORD God, and this is the altar of burnt offering for Israel"* (1 Chronicles 22:1–19).

The First Temple: Solomon's Temple

The crowning achievement of King Solomon's reign was the erection of a magnificent temple in Jerusalem, often called **Solomon's Temple** or the **First Temple**. Solomon began building the temple *"where the LORD had appeared to his father David, at the place David had prepared on the threshing floor of Araunah the Jebusite."*

Solomon's Temple was on Mount Moriah, built on the *Temple Mount*, a leveled area of approximately 35 acres. Upon completion, this temple became the center of religious worship in Israel. The Hebrew scriptures record that Solomon's Temple was an incredible achievement, built through the labors of approximately 180,000 workers, artists, and craftsmen.

The Book of Deuteronomy states that this was the sole place of Israelite *korban*, a variety of sacrificial offerings, described and commanded in the Torah. A fascinating fact concerning the building of the temple was that there was little construction noise because the stones were prepared at a quarry located far away from the building site (1 Kings 6:7).

Solomon's temple had an inside ceiling that was 180 feet long, 90 feet wide, and 50 feet tall. The highest point on the temple was 120 cubits tall (about 20 stories or about 207 feet). The construction and dedication of the temple are described in 1 Kings 6:1–38 and chapters 7–8.

Until the first temple was destroyed by the Babylonians some four hundred years later in 586 BC, sacrifice was the predominant mode of divine service. Seventy years later, another temple was completed on the same site, and sacrifices resumed. The **Book of Ezra** chronicles the building of this temple.

Many sources today refer to the temple as the **Temple of Zerubbabel** because he helped coordinate its reconstruction (Haggai 1:1). Zerubbabel ("zer-ro-ba-bell") was the leader of the tribe of Judah and part of the first wave of Jewish captives to return to Jerusalem from Persia. The Persian king Cyrus appointed Zerubbabel governor of Judah, and Zerubbabel began rebuilding the temple with the help of Joshua, the high priest (Ezra 3:2–8).

It took Zerubbabel two years to rebuild the temple's foundation, and hostile Samaritan settlers delayed construction. As a result of the opposition to the temple construction, Persia withdrew support for the project, and for more than fifteen years the temple was unfinished (Ezra 4:21). Finally, God sent the prophets **Haggai** and **Zechariah** to encourage and support Zerubbabel, and the work on the second temple resumed. Four years later, in 515 BC, the temple was completed, dedicated with great fanfare, and used to observe the Passover (Ezra 6:19).

While building this temple, a group of Jews expressed their disappointment that it did not have the size and grandeur of the first temple. It was true that Zerubbabel's temple was built on a smaller scale, but Haggai prophesied that the second temple would one day have a magnificence to outshine the glory of the first (Haggai 2:3–9). Haggai's words were fulfilled

500 years later when Jesus Christ arrived on the scene and walked on the temple steps (Luke 2:46).

King Herod's Temple

The Second Temple

Over the next four hundred years, there were many problems, and in a battle in 39 BC, King Herod took control of the temple, slaughtering many of the defenders and priests in the process. Herod wanted to renovate the temple because it was sixty cubits shorter than Solomon's original. The main work on the temple was completed in one and a half years, and the outer courtyard in eight years (63 AD). Herod's Temple was a restoration and expansion of Zerubbabel's second temple.

Herod's Temple sat on the eastern edge of Jerusalem, just west of Gethsemane and northwest of the Kidron Valley. The dimensions of Herod's Temple court were 1,550 feet by 1,000 feet. On the far northwest corner sat *Antonia Fortress*, the home of the temple garrison that prevented disturbances within the temple. Two gates provided entry into the court from the south; four from the west; and one, the *Golden Gate*, from the east. There was also an underground passage leading to the court from *Antonia Fortress*. Just inside the walls ran *porticoes* (*roofed walkways flanked on the outside by the great walls*) and the inside by rows of tall marble pillars. Tunnels passed through and into a honeycombed underground area called "*Solomon's Stable.*"

More stairs led up to the southern section of the *Court of the Gentiles*. It was at the eastern portico that the twelve-year-old Jesus debated with the scholars (Luke 2:46). It's possible that the highest corner of the east wall was where Satan took Jesus (Matthew 4:5).

Herod's temple sat skewed in the center of the large courtyard so that its entrance might better face due east towards the rising sun. Easterly facing temples were unique to the Hebrew religion of Judaism, while most pagan temples were oriented in other directions.

A balustrade (*a low wall of stone posts and caps*) defined the inner boundary of the *Court of Gentiles*, where Gentiles could worship. It was also in this court that Jesus drove out the money changers and those who were selling animals (Matthew 21:12). It was unlawful for any Gentile to go past the balustrade, an offense punishable by death.

Within the *Court of the Gentiles* was the *Court of the Women*, accessed through the *Beautiful Gate*. Here were thirteen trumpet-shaped containers for voluntary offerings. A widow donated her last two mites into one of these, an act that Jesus noticed (Mark 12:41-44).

On the west side of the *Court of the Women* were fifteen steps that led up to the *Gate of Nicanor*, where Mary brought the Baby Jesus at the time of His presentation (Luke 2:22-24). Passing through the *Nicanor Gate* would lead one into the *Court of Israel*, accessible only to ceremonially clean Jewish men. A low balustrade and another staircase separated the *Court of Israel* from the *Court of the Priests*; three gates, one each from the south, west, and north, provided priests more direct access from the outer courtyard.

Alter of Sacrifice in the Court of the Priests

In the *Court of Priests* was the altar for the burnt offerings. The altar was forty feet on each side, twenty feet high, and made of uncarved stone (unhewn). The nearby area where the animals were slaughtered was fitted with a trough of running water, fed by a spring and underground cisterns to wash away the blood. Also in the *Court of Priests* was a large basin called *the Brazen Sea or the Laver*, resting upon twelve bulls cast in bronze. Beyond these fixtures was another staircase leading to a curtain embroidered with a map of the known world covering the temple entrance. Only the priest on duty was allowed to advance beyond that curtain.

Inside Herod's temple, the setup resembled that of the Tabernacle of Moses. Beyond the first veil was a hall containing the golden altar of incense, the golden table of showbread, and the golden lampstand. It was this lampstand, the seven-armed menorah, that was said to have somehow stayed lit during the eight-day rededication of the temple after the Maccabean victory in the second century BC.

Only the high priest could pass beyond the final veil to the Holy of Holies, and then only once a year on the Day of Atonement. This room's floor, walls, and ceiling were plated with gold.

Because the *Ark of the Covenant* had been lost years before, Herod's temple had no furnishings in the *Holy of Holies*, although it is possible a stone held the place of the ark. It was this veil, leading into the Holy of Holies, which tore from the top down when Jesus was crucified (Matthew 27:51).

Around the Holy of Holies, to the south, west, and north, were three stories of interconnected rooms. Openings from the story immediately above the Holy of Holies allowed workers to be lowered into that room to make repairs without touching the floor.

Herod's temple lasted until 70 AD, and at that time, after a long war between the Jewish Zealots and the Roman authorities, four Roman legions, led by *Titus*, attacked Jerusalem and burned down the temple. As the temple burned, the gold and silver ornamentation melted and seeped between the cracks in the stones. The Roman soldiers took the temple apart, stone by stone, to get this bounty, thus fulfilling Jesus' prophecy (Matthew 24:1-3).

> **"And Jesus went out, and departed from the temple: and his disciples came to him for to shew him the buildings of the temple. And Jesus said unto them, See ye not all these things? verily I say unto you, There shall not be left here one stone upon another, that shall not be thrown down."**

The Jewish people were scattered and did not return in masse to Israel until after World War II. The *Temple Mount*, where Herod's temple stood, is now home to the Islamic *Dome of the Rock (the iconic golden dome)*. All that remains today of Herod's work on the Temple Mount is the *Western Wall* (the Wailing Wall), where Jews pray. This is a 1,600-foot-extended portion of the retaining wall Herod had constructed to expand the Temple Mount.

The Temple Mount is the holiest site in *Judaism*, the third-holiest site in *Islam*, and a revered site to *Christians*. The Jews call it *Har HaMoriyah* (Mount Moriah) and *Har HaBayit* (Temple Mount). The site is known to Muslims as Haram al-Sharif (The Sacred Noble Sanctuary). Christians refer to it as *Mount Zion*.

After the 1967 Six-Day War, during which the Temple Mount was captured, control of the Temple Mount was turned over to the Jordanian Waqf. In establishing a Waqf, the donor (*waqīf*) dedicates the assets (*mawqūf*) for a specific charitable purpose. According to Sharia Law, once a property is designated as Waqf, there can be no possibility of transfer of ownership, not through inheritance, sale, or otherwise. Waqf properties are also exempt from taxes.

Because the site is important to three major religions, its ownership is hotly contested. Islam teaches that Mohammed made a miraculous night journey from Mecca to Jerusalem in 621 AD (Quran, Surah 17:1). He led worship at "the farthest mosque," was lifted to heaven, and returned to earth to carry on his teachings.

At that time, there was no mosque in Jerusalem, but 15 years later, Caliph Umar built a small mosque to commemorate the Prophet's night visit. The Al Aqsa Mosque, "the farthest mosque," was built in 705 AD and rebuilt in 754, 780, and 1035.

The *Dome of the Rock* was built in 692 AD over the place where Mohammad supposedly ascended to heaven. Christians and Jews also identify this site as the place where Abraham offered Isaac as a sacrifice and the location of the Holy of Holies in the Jewish temple. At this exact location, God led Solomon to build the First Temple, Zerubbabel rebuilt the Second Temple, and Herod the Great enlarged it in 12 BC.

The Church will one day be *raptured* out of this world to meet the Lord in the air. Shortly thereafter, the 70th week of Daniel's prophecy will begin (Daniel 9:24-27). These seven years are referred to as the Tribulation. God intends to discipline Israel for her sins under the Mosaic Covenant and lead the nation to repent and turn to Christ. It is a period of God's judgment upon the earth in preparation for the return of the Messiah, Jesus Christ.

The Third Temple
Scripture states that the Antichrist will rise to power on the earth, and he will promise Israel and the Jewish people something for which they have longed for centuries—peace. He will ensure peace through a covenant confirmed with Israel for seven years.

After three and a half years, drastic changes will occur, and the Antichrist will break the covenant. He will enter the Temple, desecrate its altar by placing an image of himself there, and demand that the Jewish people worship him as God (Daniel 9:27; 11:36). He will also stop all sacrifices in the temple. But if future "daily sacrifices" are going to be stopped, they must first be resumed.

Construction for this third temple may be started or even completed during the Tribulation timeframe, or possibly a bit earlier, just before the Rapture of the Church. Once this temple is built and dedicated, the Levitical system of sacrifices could be reinstituted. Many Old Covenant rituals require a tabernacle or temple to be consistent with God's Law, referred to as the Mosaic or Old Covenant.

Since the destruction of the Second Temple in 70 AD, the Jewish People can no longer offer their sacrifices. It's stated that 202 out of the **613 *mitzvot*** (commandments) in the Torah cannot be performed without a Temple. With no Temple in Jerusalem, the Jewish people now worship the God of Israel in their local community synagogues and through the study of Torah. Instead of offering animal sacrifices, they now offer

Tefillah (prayer), *Teshuvah* (repentance), and *Tzedakah* (charity).

Daniel 12:11 states that many of these events will occur at "*the time of the end,*" and that "*from the time that the daily sacrifice is taken away, and the abomination of desolation is set up, there shall be one thousand two hundred and ninety days*"— indicating a countdown to Jesus Christ's return. Many see this scripture as a sign that a temple must be built in Jerusalem before Christ returns.

In 2 Thessalonians 2:4, the Apostle Paul wrote about the Antichrist:

"Who opposeth and exalteth himself above all that is called God, or that is worshipped; so that he as God sitteth in the temple of God, shewing himself that he is God."

In the *Olivet Discourse*, Jesus referred to the restored temple and its desecration:

"When you see the 'abomination of desolation,' spoken of by Daniel the prophet, standing in the holy place... then let those who are in Judea flee to the mountains.... For then there will be great tribulation, such as has not been since the beginning of the world until this time, no, nor ever shall be" (Matthew 24:15–16).

So, does a third temple have to be built, or will an altar for the sacrifices be sufficient? After the destruction of Solomon's temple and before Zerubbabel, Jews returned to Jerusalem and resumed sacrifices to God (Ezra 3:1-2). This shows that only an altar was necessary for sacrifices, and a temple was not required. While it is possible that the Jews will build another temple before the return of Christ, it is also possible that the Jews will begin offering sacrifices on an altar without building a temple.

But once again we are reminded that Jesus spoke of an end-time "*Abomination of Desolation*" that would stand "in the holy place" before His return (Matthew 24:15). Many believe the phrase "*holy place*" means there will be another temple. However, this phrase could also refer to an altar on the Temple Mount.

Another obstacle to building a third temple is the attitude of the Jewish people and their leaders. The average Israeli knows that any attempt to make a third temple on the Dome of the Rock would result in immediate war with the Muslims. Something will have to happen to create a surge of nationalistic pride that will demand a new temple. Could this catalytic event possibly lead to the discovery of the Ark of the Covenant?

The building of a third temple by the Jews on the Temple Mount is indeed shrouded in uncertainty and is a focal point of Arab Israeli anger. When Jesus died the veil that separated the people from the Holy of Holies was torn in two from the top to the bottom, signifying that the separation and division of the old system was done (Matthew 27:51). Also, the Apostle Paul writes that Jesus put the Law, the Old Covenant, to death on that cross (Colossians 2:14). The Temple system was part of that covenant. We are of the New Covenant.

Everything seems ready for the building of the Third Temple, except the land on which to build it. Since the liberation of the Mount in 1967, the Muslim world has made great efforts to claim the entire 35-acre platform as its own sacred land. But only an incredibly gifted man will be able to establish a peace plan that allows both Muslims and Jews to worship the Lord in the same temple. Could this man be the Antichrist?

Another issue is that a few Israeli archaeologists have challenged where the Jewish Temple once stood. Some suggest that the location is wrong because Roman constructions took up space on the Temple Mount, and the Temple itself was further down in the area known as the City of David. The City of David is just south of the Temple Mount area and outside the walls of the Old City as it stands today. The city was also known as Salem, where Melchizedek came from in Abraham's time.

Another thought is that the ancient temples were located north of the Dome and that the sacrificial altar inside the Dome was the one that Solomon built in *"the middle of the court"* to handle the thousands of extraordinary sacrifices he offered to the Lord on the day the Temple was dedicated. At this dedication, King Solomon offered a sacrifice of twenty-two thousand bulls and one hundred and twenty thousand sheep (2 Chronicles 7:5).

If this thought is actual, the Third Temple could be built north of the Dome of the Rock. This may well be the solution the Antichrist comes up with when he negotiates a peace covenant between the Jews and the Arabs (Daniel 9:27).

The **Temple Institute** and the **Temple Mount and Eretz Yisrael Faithful Movement** are the two main Jewish organizations responsible for preparing for the Third Temple and reinstating sacrificial worship. The Institute aims to see Israel rebuild the Holy Temple on Mount Moriah in Jerusalem. It is thought that the Third Temple will *"bring the Light back into the world,"* which left the Temple Mount when the Lord's Divine Presence departed.

In 2015, these groups completed an altar needed to restart sacrifices and performed a re-enactment of the *Passover* sacrifice. In 2017, they performed a sacrifice near the Temple Mount, a controversial act that resulted in some being arrested. In 2018, they were permitted to re-enact the Passover sacrifice at the foot of the Temple Mount. Later, they made a somewhat unusual announcement that five red heifers were flown to Israel from a Christian group in Texas to meet the requirements for resuming temple sacrifices.

A heifer is a young female cow that has not yet calved. This requirement comes from Numbers 19:2-10, where God commanded a sacrifice of this special heifer whose ashes would be used for *"the water of purification,"* necessary to purify the priests before they could offer sacrifices.

Ritual garments and gold and copper vessels have also been created, such as the abuv, a three-tiered stand used for roasting the Omer, an ancient Israelite unit of dry measure on

Passover. Coal will be used for roasting barley, and copper vessels will be used to prepare the meal offering.

Even a reconstruction of the 24-carat golden Menorah, the seven-branched candelabra, has been crafted. According to Jewish history, the Roman legions took the Menorah to Rome, Italy, in 70 AD, when the temple was destroyed.

Other items created are Levitical musical instruments, such as Silver Trumpets, Lyres (a stringed instrument of the harp class having an approximately U-shaped frame), and Harps, to worship the Lord, just as King David did 3,000 years ago (1 Chronicles 23:5).

Cedar from Lebanon, captured in the north during the war in 1982, has also been stored for the next temple. The Temple Institute's School is training certified, DNA-tested Cohen descendants of the High Priest Aaron to perform the Temple duties. Some reports state that it would only take 9 to 12 months to completely build the third Temple, as most of it has already been fabricated.

Today's Muslim-Palestinian narrative maintains that the two biblical Jewish temples in Jerusalem never existed—a blatant denial of historical accounts in the Bible:

> *"There has never been a Jewish temple atop the Temple Mount,"* states Sheikh Muhammad Ahmad Hussein, grand mufti of Jerusalem.

Such statements contradict the Qur'an. According to the Qur'an (chapter 17), at least one biblical temple existed—Solomon's. Also, Muslim tradition holds that the early form of the Aksa Mosque was built deliberately on the verified site of earlier sanctuaries: "The mosque was itself a revivification of the old Jewish temple."

Along with the rebuilding of the temple, we also need to remember that the Jewish nation does not currently occupy all the territory of the Promised Land, which would include present-day Israel, Lebanon, the West Bank of Jordan, and substantial portions of Syria, Iraq, and Saudi Arabia. Israel fulfilled numerous prophecies when it returned to its homeland in 1948, but to this day, the land mentioned above is still in question.

Based on end time scripture, it is thought that the Third Temple will have a limited lifetime and be destroyed by a great earthquake as the Mount of Olives splits in half (Zechariah 14:4). This will occur at the second coming of Jesus Christ. The specific identity of the Antichrist will not be revealed to the world until the peace treaty with Israel is broken. The Holy Spirit, the restrainer, lives in the world now in the members of the Church, but some believe He will leave the earth when the Church itself is removed at the Rapture.

Keep in mind that God has sovereignty over all world affairs. Israel is still God's chosen people, and the Tribulation will take place to humble and purify Israel. The people of Israel will eventually enjoy all the blessings that God has promised. We talk of a third temple, but the next event on God's prophetic timeline is thought to be the Rapture of the Church. This could happen at any time.

Jesus said, **"Therefore you also be ready, for the Son of Man is coming at an hour you do not expect"** (Matthew 24:44).

The Millennial Temple

We are told of a fourth temple that will be built, the Millennial Temple. At the end of the Tribulation, Jesus Christ will return to earth in all His glory and establish His 1,000–year reign. A glorious Millennial Temple will be constructed, far surpassing the Temples built by Solomon, Zerubbabel, and Herod.

The Prophet Ezekiel said, **"The Lord said that this Temple will be the place of my throne, and the place of the soles of my feet, where I will dwell in the midst of the children of Israel forever"** (Ezekiel 43:7). Jerusalem will be known as "The Lord Is There," so this temple will stand at a time when Jesus is ruling in Jerusalem. This magnificent temple will tower above the skyline and be Jerusalem's focal point. Ezekiel gives very exacting measurements of this building, which are summarized (Ezekiel 42:15-20).

The Temple area will measure 500 reeds on each of its four sides (a reed is approximately ten feet). Therefore, the Millennial Temple will be approximately one mile square. It will be the largest and most magnificent structure ever erected, and it will all be for the glory of God. Significant topographical changes will be needed to accommodate the size of the temple and its outer areas.

"For in mine holy mountain, in the mountain of the height of Israel, saith the Lord God, there shall all the house of Israel, all of those in the land, serve me" (Ezekiel 20:40).

The Prophet Isaiah stated, *"And it shall come to pass in the last days, that the mountain of the LORD's house shall be established in the top of the mountains, and shall be exalted above the hills; and all nations shall flow unto it. And many people shall go and say, Come ye, and let us go up to the mountain of the LORD, to the house of the God of Jacob"* (Isaiah 2:1-3).

Present-day Jerusalem, which is 2,500 feet above sea level, is not large enough to contain the future Temple area spoken of in the Scriptures. But as usual, God has a plan. Zechariah indicates that at least three significant geological and topographical changes will occur when the Messiah returns to the earth at His Second Advent.

"On that day his feet will stand on the Mount of Olives, east of Jerusalem, and the <u>Mount of Olives will be split in two from east to west</u>, forming a great valley, with half of the mountain moving north and half moving south. You will flee by my mountain valley, for it will extend to Azel. You will flee as you fled from the earthquake in the days of Uzziah king of Judah. Then the Lord my God will come, and all the holy ones with him. On that day <u>living water will flow out from Jerusalem,</u>

half of it east to the Dead Sea and half of it west to the Mediterranean Sea, in summer and in winter. All the land shall be turned like the Arabah from Geba to Rimmon south of Jerusalem; and it, Jerusalem, shall be lifted up, and inhabited in its place, from Benjamin's gate unto the place of the first gate, unto the corner gate, and from the tower of Hananel unto the king's wine presses" (Zechariah 14:4-10).

Jerusalem will not only be raised as a high mountain, but it will also be significantly enlarged. The holy part of the land will be immense, measuring 25,000 by 25,000 reeds. (This area is 50 X 50 miles, or about 2,500 square miles). It will be the center of the worship of God (Ezekiel 45:1). The northern section will be 50 X 20 miles. In the center of that section will stand the Temple, which will be one mile square, and a segment of priests will live in the rest of the area. The central portion, also 50 X 20 miles, will be reserved for the Levites, with the southern section of 50 X 10 miles reserved for building the Millennial Jerusalem (10 X 10 miles) and growing food.

For centuries, the glory of God had been with Israel. He led them in their wilderness journeys and was in the Tabernacles and Temples, but because of their idolatry and turning away from the Lord, the Shekinah glory of God left them (1 Samuel 4:21). But now, in his vision of the Millennial Temple, Ezekiel was privileged to see the glory of God return to the city and His people and gives a breathtaking account of the glory of God returning through the Eastern Gate.

Jesus will return to this new Temple and dwell in the inner court (Ezekiel 43:4-5). The priests in this Millennial Temple will be from the sons of Zadok (Ezekiel 40:46). They alone, of all the Levites, remained faithful to the Lord in David's time (2 Samuel 15:24-29). Zadok's reward will be access to God's presence and the privilege of ministering in all phases of the priestly duties.

Sacrifices will be offered in this magnificent Temple. Why sacrifices? Doesn't the Book of Hebrews teach that Christ's sacrificial, atoning death was once and for all and totally sufficient? The answers to these questions have long been the subject of controversy. Some say that these future sacrifices will be a continuous memorial to the work of Christ on the cross. They will in no way detract from His redeeming work at Calvary. Nothing can do that.

Likewise, since Christ instituted it the night before His crucifixion, the Church has celebrated the Lord's Supper as a memorial of His death. This does not detract from the cross but is a constant reminder of what Christ did for us. However, the sacrifices are for atonement rather than memorial (Ezekiel 45:15-20).

Many Jews acknowledge from the **Tanakh** that the shedding of blood is associated with the remission of sins. Thus, restoring animal sacrifices in a properly consecrated temple is important to them. Others say that the sacrifices could have been a temporary ceremonial purification during Jesus's 1,000-year reign.

Although the world is at peace and Satan is bound so that he can no longer deceive the nations, it is not utopia (Revelation 20.3). Many survivors of the Tribulation, and their descendants, will be unsaved, and man himself will still have a rebellious heart. This will be a partial population of unglorified humanity.

Later, many of these inhabitants of the New Jerusalem will be glorified and not be a source of impurities that defile Yahweh's holiness. Sacrifices will not be a return to the Mosaic Law since the Law has been forever fulfilled and discontinued through the work of Christ.

It is helpful to remind ourselves that the Millennial scenario is considered "very Jewish." People will come from all over the world to worship Christ in His Temple. Jewish feasts and rituals, such as the Feast of Tabernacles, will be honored since some Jewish festivals are to be held as "statutes forever."

John is shown the **New Jerusalem** in the **New Heavens/New Earth**:

"And I heard a great voice out of heaven saying, Behold, the tabernacle of God is with men, and he will dwell with them, and they shall be his people, and God himself shall be with them, and be their God. And God shall wipe away all tears from their eyes; and there shall be no more death, neither sorrow, nor crying, neither shall there be any more pain: for the former things are passed away. And he that sat upon the throne said, Behold, I make all things new" (Revelation 21).

According to scripture, the New Jerusalem will descend from Heaven when New Heaven and New Earth are created. The Apostle John says that there will be no temple in New Jerusalem.

"And I saw no temple therein: for the Lord God Almighty and the Lamb are the temple of it. And the city had no need of the sun, neither of the moon, to shine in it: for the glory of God did lighten it, and the Lamb is the light thereof" (Revelation 21:22-23).

From scripture, prophecy, and the very throne of God, we have the declaration that God's home, city, and people are now with Him for eternity.

Babylon

An ancient city located in Shinar, in ancient Mesopotamia, on  the eastern bank of the Euphrates River. King Nimrod founded it and its earliest act of defiance was building the Tower of Babel. The Bible first mentions Babylon in Genesis 11 as a place of rebellion against God. This chapter introduces a significant moment in human history, where humanity, speaking one language, builds a tower to reach the heavens in defiance of God's command. Their unity leads to God's intervention, scattering them across the earth and confounding their language.

In 2 Kings 17:7, we see that Israel had turned from God, ignored His prophets, and worshiped idols; so God handed them over to the Assyrians. Judah followed Israel's example so God would bring a similar fate upon them, but this time, He would discipline them through the Babylonians.

Ezekiel chapter 21 describes a scene within the kingdom of Judah. King Zedekiah, the last king of Judah, is seated on his throne in the royal palace in Jerusalem. The prophet Ezekiel stands before the king and delivers a message from the Lord. He speaks of the impending destruction of Jerusalem and the fall of the kingdom of Judah at the hands of the Babylonians.

Babylon was the nation God used to judge Israel, sending them into exile beginning in 605 BC and destroying the temple in 586 BC. Babylon was arguably the first kingdom to have a global influence. Even after its fall in roughly 539 BC, Babylon continued to be seen as a place of evil.

Babylon is continually portrayed as a wicked city in Christian scriptures and is associated with the Babylonian exile in Hebrew scriptures. Its meaning—"Gate of God"—also places it as a city or place of incredible luxury, sensuality, and often vice and corruption. The prophet Daniel was one of the young men taken to Babylon as an exile, and he rose to prominence in the administration of King Nebuchadnezzar.

Babylon figures prominently in the book of Revelation as the ultimate enemy of God and persecutor of His people. **"Babylon the Great"** will be overthrown. For years, many dispensationalists have interpreted Babylon in the Bible as Rome, the center of a revived Roman Empire. With Saddam Hussein's ascendency and the war in Iraq, many changed their interpretation, thinking that Babylon might refer to a revived Babylonian Empire. Saddam Hussein tried to rebuild Babylon and even fancied himself the new Nebuchadnezzar. However, as events unfolded, it became clear that Hussein was not God's final enemy and that he would not successfully restore a Babylonian Empire.

Babylon, as the enemy of God, can be seen as:

1. A literal city
2. A worldwide system of government, trade, and entertainment
3. A spiritual entity

All three must be considered together to understand Babylon. The Apostle John, while in exile on the island of Patmos, had a vision, and an angel spoke to him:

"Then the angel carried me away in the Spirit into a wilderness. There I saw a woman sitting on a scarlet beast that was covered with blasphemous names and had seven heads and ten horns. The woman was dressed in purple and scarlet, and was glittering with gold, precious stones and pearls. She held a golden cup in her hand, filled with abominable things and the filth of her adulteries. The name written on her forehead was a mystery: Babylon the Great, the mother of prostitutes and of the abominations of the earth. I saw that the woman was drunk with the blood of God's holy people, the blood of those who bore testimony to Jesus" (Revelation 17:3-6).

Perhaps the mystery of the whore of Babylon can be partially solved. The desolate **wilderness** may symbolize spiritual barrenness and separation from God.

The **woman** defined as the **"whore of Babylon"** may represent a corrupt and deceptive entity, possibly symbolizing unfaithfulness or the spirit of seduction working in the world.

The **scarlet beast** symbolizes power, perhaps a force being manipulated by the deceitful woman. Together, they create an image of a dangerous alliance between seduction and authority. The woman being "full of blasphemous names" signifies defiance and rebellion against God.

The **seven heads** symbolize seven political powers or empires that have been instrumental in carrying out Satan's opposition to God's plan. These heads are generally interpreted as representing **successive empires** that have persecuted God's people throughout history. They include Egypt, Assyria, Babylon, Medo-Persia, Greece, Pagan Rome, and Papal Rome—a continuation of the Roman Empire in a religious form often identified with the Papacy. The *whore of Babylon* is closely associated with the end-times **Antichrist**.

The fact that she is referred to as a **mystery** means that we cannot be sure about her identity. *"This calls for a mind with wisdom"* (Revelation 17:9).

"The ten horns are ten kings who will come from this kingdom" (Daniel 7:24). *"The ten horns you saw are ten kings who have not yet received a kingdom, but who for one hour will receive authority as kings along with the beast. They will wage war against the Lamb"* (Rev 17:12-13).

The Antichrist is the beast that will hold political power during the Tribulation. Perhaps the Antichrist will rise from a "revived" Roman Empire in the last days. That empire will be divided into ten parts and governed by ten kings who will rule under the Antichrist. These ten kings, symbolized as horns, voluntarily cede authority to the one-world leader, the Antichrist. They will wage war against Jesus (the Lamb) and His people.

"Then I saw the beast and the kings of the earth and their armies gathered together to wage war against the rider on the horse and his army. But the beast was captured, and with it the false prophet. The two of them were thrown alive into the fiery lake of burning sulfur" (Revelation 19:19-20).

So back to the reference of the *whore of Babylon and a city*. This does not necessarily stand for a resurrection of ancient Babylon, which fell to Cyrus the Great in 539 BC. Some feel that the city is Rome. However, she has been variously identified with Jerusalem, non-Christian religions, Russia, the United States, and even the Roman Catholic Church.

In Revelation 17:5, we see that this woman is dressed in expensive, fine apparel. On her forehead is her identity:

"BABYLON THE GREAT, THE MOTHER OF PROSTITUTES AND OF THE ABOMINATIONS OF THE EARTH."

The angel who speaks to John identifies Babylon the Great as *"the great city that rules over the kings of the earth."*

So, what does the term **"Babylon the Great"** really mean? Some say it's a figurative reference to the great powers of ancient Rome. This view is known as *"preterism,"* meaning that some or all prophecies of the Bible have already been fulfilled in history. Others would argue that Babylon the Great is used as a figure of speech about evil nations in general. Some think the term means a revived and rebuilt Babylon. But the Book of Revelation sees **Babylon the Great as an evil world system, controlled by the Antichrist during the last days before Jesus' return**. We learned that Babylon the Great will influence all people, multitudes, nations, and languages. She will promote religious heresy and will be *"drunk with the blood of many of God's holy people"* and will actively lead people astray. Be mindful that the fall of Babylon the Great results from God's judgment as He works through the ten kings to carry out His will (Revelation 17:16-18).

> *"The 10 horns you saw, and the beast, will hate the prostitute. They will make her desolate and naked, devour her flesh, and burn her up with fire. For God has put it into their hearts to carry out His plan by having one purpose and to give their kingdom to the beast until God's words are accomplished. And the woman you saw is the great city that has an empire over the kings of the earth."*

In the end, the kingdoms that Babylon the Great relied on would turn against her, and when she was no longer needed, the beast and the ten kings would dispose of her. John then heard the loud voice of a great multitude in heaven saying, *"Alleluia! God has judged the great harlot. Her smoke rises up forever and ever!"* (Revelation 19:1-3).

The end times will be horrific. The Antichrist's system will be characterized by rampant materialism, love of money, outrageous idolatry, religious sacrilege, and violence against Christians. However, at the end of the Tribulation, Babylon the Great will be destroyed. The Antichrist and the False Prophet will be *"thrown alive into the fiery lake of burning sulfur"* (Revelation 19:20), and Satan will be cast into the abyss for 1000 years. At the end of the Millennium, he will be released to deceive the nations again. He will gather many for battle, and they will attack Jerusalem. Fire will come down from heaven and devour them all. Satan and all unbelievers will join the Antichrist and False Prophet in the Lake of Fire for an eternity of torment. Jesus will reign over all creation as the **"King of Kings and Lord of Lords."** He will have supreme authority and sovereignty.

This study reminds us to seek fulfillment in God rather than in the world's corrupt systems. We can navigate a world of evil and temptations by aligning our lives with God's truth and love.

The Two Witnesses

God will have Two Witnesses stand before the Antichrist, the world's political leader. *"And I will appoint my two witnesses, and they will prophesy for 1,260 days, clothed in sackcloth"* (Revelation 11:1-12). These two witnesses will have the power to shut  up the heavens so that it will not rain, turn the waters into blood, and strike the earth with every kind of plague as often as they want.

There are three primary theories on the identity of the two witnesses in Revelation: (1) **Moses and Elijah**, (2) **Enoch and Elijah**, and (3) **two unknown believers** whom God calls to be His witnesses in the end times.

Moses and Elijah are possibilities due to the specific miracles John says the witnesses will perform.

> "They have power to shut up the heavens so that it will not rain during the time they are prophesying; and they have power to turn the waters into blood and to strike the earth with every kind of plague as often as they want" (Revelation 11:6).

Moses turned the Nile River into blood (Exodus 7), Elijah destroyed his enemies with fire (2 Kings 1), and Moses and Elijah both appeared with Jesus at the Transfiguration (Matthew 17:3-4).

Enoch and Elijah are seen as possibilities because they were taken by God directly to heaven without experiencing death. In Elijah's case, "*As they were walking along and talking together, suddenly a chariot of fire and horses of fire appeared and separated the two of them, and Elijah went up to heaven in a whirlwind*" (2 Kings 2:11). As for Enoch, "*Enoch walked faithfully with God; then he was no more, because God took him away*" (Genesis 5:24).

Proponents of this viewpoint look to (Hebrews 9:27), which says that **all men are appointed to die once**. The fact that neither Enoch nor Elijah has yet experienced death seems to qualify them for the job of the two witnesses who will be killed on earth when their job is done. In addition, both Enoch and Elijah were prophets who pronounced God's judgment (1 Kings 17:1, Jude 1:14-15).

However, it could be that the two witnesses are **two unknown people** who were not identified in the scripture. God can certainly take two "ordinary" believers and enable them to perform the same signs and wonders that Moses and Elijah did. Perhaps Zechariah 3 and 4 may give a hint about these two witnesses.

After the Jewish people experienced exile in Babylon, King Cyrus of Persia allowed 50,000 of them to return to Jerusalem to rebuild the temple under the direction of Zerubbabel, governor of Jerusalem. God delivered a message to the prophet Zechariah: *"This is the word of the LORD to Zerubbabel: Not by might, nor by power, but by my Spirit, says the LORD of hosts."* The work of rebuilding the temple would only be accomplished by God's Spirit and not by human might or power.

The prophet had a vision and saw two olive trees providing oil to a solid gold lampstand, which continually gave off its light. An angel tells Zechariah: *"The two olive trees are the two anointed ones who stand by the Lord of the whole earth"* (Zechariah 4:14). In other words, God's power to sustain His work flows through two individuals set apart for this task. In Zechariah's view, these two individuals were **Joshua,** the current high priest, and **Zerubbabel**, the current governor of Judah. The Joshua mentioned here is a Levite and a descendant of Aaron. He helped rebuild the temple and was not the Joshua who assisted Moses.

The apostle John then describes the two witnesses in Revelation 11:4: *"They are the two olive trees and the two lampstands, and they stand before the Lord of the earth."* The Holy Spirit will empower them. So, who are the Two Witnesses of Revelation? Scripture doesn't tell us, but they will be mighty men.

Christianity and Islam

The word ***Allah*** has been used by Arabic people of different religions since pre-Islamic times. The origin of the title Allah goes back before Muhammad, who found that the Meccans worshipped a supreme deity whom they called Allah, along with a host of lesser gods. Although Allah has become known as the proper name for the Muslim god, Allah is not a name but a descriptor that means literally *"the god."*

Many rituals performed in the name of Allah relate to the pagan worship that existed before Islam. This deity has the sacred idol temple at **Mecca** called *"the House of Allah" (Ka'aba),* which contains the Black Stone and is dedicated to worshipping Allah only. The oldest name of the moon god was **"Sin"** (of Sumerian origin), and the father of the sun god was **"Shamash."** While the Arabs worshipped 360 gods at the Kaaba in Mecca, the Moon-god was the chief deity. The Moon-God was also called *Ilah,* which eventually became **Allah***.* The Crescent Moon is the symbol of Islam, and the month-long *Ramadan* fasting begins and ends with the crescent moon.

Muhammad and Islam: Muhammad was from Mecca, a city near the Red Sea in what is now Saudi Arabia. He was an orphan raised by an uncle and later became a merchant. Over time, Muhammad decided that the moon God Allah was not only the greatest god, but the only god. Islam was founded by Muhammad, who Muslims consider to be Seal of the Prophets and the earthly manifestation of primordial light (Nūr) emanated by God. Muhammad stated that while praying in a cave, he was visited by the angel **Gabriel***,* who supposedly gave Muhammad revelations from Allah. It is thought that this continued for about 23 years until Muhammad's death. Muhammad proclaimed that "God is One," that there is no Trinity, and that Jesus was simply another prophet, along with Adam, Noah, Abraham, Moses, and David.

He also taught that complete surrender is the only way to please Allah. **Islam** means "peaceful, willing submission to God's guidance." The Arabic word **"*salam*"** also means peace. The word **Muslim** means *"one who submits to Allah"* or *"a follower of the religion of Islam."* Muslims credit Muhammad with restoring the "true" religion of Islam to a world that had corrupted it.

Muhammad had many conflicts with the Meccan tribes, but he gathered 10,000 converts over time and took over **Mecca**. He and his followers then set out to destroy all pagan temples in western Arabia, and they succeeded. The rest of Muhammad's life was devoted to promoting and growing

Islam throughout the Arab world. Sometimes Muhammad used his wealth from plundering to bribe people into Islam, while at other times he used threats and terrorism. You would have the choice of accepting Islam or being killed.

After Muhammad's death, his revelations were compiled and canonized into what is now called the **Qur'an**—the Muslim holy book. Islamic and Arabic scholars say the spelling Qur'an is preferred, but in much of the non-Arab world, it is more commonly spelled Quran or Koran.

The Qur'an is the foundational text of Islam, and through the **Islamic Sharia,** it shapes legal systems, politics, ethics, cultures, and worship for much of the world's population. Muslims believe this book is God's final Word and is perfect and holy. It is divided into 114 chapters called **surahs**. Like the Bible, some things about the Qur'an are hard to understand and seem puzzling, but the text draws heavily upon the Bible.

The two most often named figures in the Qur'an are Moses (136 times) and Abraham (69 times). Jesus is mentioned by name six times, as often as Muhammad.

John of Damascus, writing a century after Muhammad, claimed that Muhammad, after conversing with an Arian monk concerning the Old and New Testament, fabricated his own heresy, which is why many Bible scriptures are found in the Qur'an. Islam holds that the **Torah** (the first five books of the Old Testament), the Psalms, and the Gospels were given by God, but the Jews and Christians have corrupted God's Word, and therefore, the Bible cannot be fully trusted. In addition to the Qur'an, the Muslims have the **Hadith**, a collection of Muhammad's sayings, opinions, and actions as reported by those close to him, and the **Tafsir**, which is a commentary of sorts on the Qur'an.

Today, you may hear the word **Islamophobia**. This is commonly defined as an irrational fear or hatred of the Islamic religion or of Muslims. It is a fear or hatred that manifests itself in discrimination and is often used to smear anyone who disagrees with any part of the Islamic religion. The danger here is that it can also produce violence and become a threat not only to religion but also to any of the good people who may be associated with it.

The GOD of the Holy Bible: The word God is found throughout the Bible, but the Lord reveals Himself more personally through the names with which He introduces Himself in Scripture. These names help people when they address Him in prayer.

The Lord (Jehovah) is my shepherd (Rohi). In Hebrew, it reads ***Jehovah-Rohi*** ("The Lord Is My Shepherd"). King David is the author of this poem (Psalm 23).

Jehovah-Jireh: The Lord Shall Provide was mentioned when the patriarch Abraham was instructed to sacrifice his promised son as a burnt offering on Mount Moriah (Genesis 22).

Jehovah-Rapha: The Lord Who Heals. This tells the story of the early days of the Israelites' travels in the wilderness (Exodus 15).

Jehovah-Nissi: The Lord Is My Banner. Moses led the children of Israel through the desert, and they met fierce enemies (Exodus 17).

Jehovah-M'Kaddesh: The Lord Who Sanctifies—"Keep my statutes and do them. I am the Lord, who sanctifies you" (Leviticus).

Jehovah-Shalom: The Lord Who Is Peace—first used by Gideon when the angel of the Lord appeared to him (Judges).

Jehovah-Tsidkenu: The Lord Who Is Righteous—speaking of a day when the Lord reigns over the nation of Israel (Jeremiah).

Jehovah-Shammah: The Lord Who Is There—symbolic meaning the Lord will always be in Jerusalem (Ezekiel).

We must also include the names: **YHWH/YAHWEH, JEHOVAH, I AM, MESSIAH, LORD, ADONAI, MASTER, ELOHIM,** and **ABBA**.

In the Hebrew Scriptures, the name of God is recorded as **YHWH**. So, one might ask: Where did the name "***Jehovah***" come from? Early Hebrew did not use vowels in its written form. The proper vowel sounds of words were passed down orally, which becomes a real issue when studying the Hebrew name of God. It is written in the Hebrew scriptures as **YHWH**, which is translated as "***Yahweh***" (YAH-way), while others use the word "***Jehovah***." Christians know that it is far more important to know God through faith in ***Jesus Christ***, than it is to know the correct pronunciation of His name in Hebrew.

Faith is necessary to please God. **"But without faith it is impossible to please him: for he that cometh to God must believe that he is, and that he is a rewarder of them that diligently seek him"** (Hebrews 11:6).

Evidence of God exists in daily human experiences. Romans 1:19-20 states:

"Since what may be known about God is plain to them because God has made it plain to them. For since the creation of the world God's invisible qualities—his eternal power and divine nature—have been clearly seen, being understood from what has been made, so that people are without excuse."

"The heavens declare the glory of God; the skies proclaim the work of his hands" (Psalms 19:1).

"He has made everything beautiful in its time. He has also set eternity in the human heart; yet no one can fathom what God has done from beginning to end and certainly in the design of the universe around us" (Ecclesiastes 3:11).

Archaeology supports the Bible since secular discoveries have repeatedly confirmed people, events, and places depicted in Scripture. These discoveries also support the existence of a faithful God. Logic tells us that it would take a sovereign God to create this huge universe and control the smallest of details, such as our birth, DNA, or even the growing of a small plant. Many changed lives and answers to prayer are all part of our personal belief that God exists. Jesus came to earth as a human being so we could have a personal relationship with God. Accepting the existence of God is like being in the darkest night and then taking a trusting step into the bright sunlight, where many things are then made clear to you.

Christianity: In Christianity, all scripture is "God-breathed," meaning that Holy Scriptures are ordained by God's authority and produced by the enabling of His Holy Spirit through the writings of human authors (2 Timothy 3:16-17). The Bible consists of several books, with the Four Gospels being eyewitness accounts of Jesus Christ's life and ministry.

The Bible warns against adding to God's Word. This is another reason that a person should be careful of the Islamic teachings.

> *"For I testify unto every man that heareth the words of the prophecy of this book, If any man shall add unto these things, God shall add unto him the plagues that are written in this book; and if any man shall take away from the words of the book of this prophecy, God shall take away his part out of the book of life, and out of the holy city, and from the things which are written in this book"* (Revelation 22:18-19).

Christianity's teachings compared to those of Islam are as different as night and day.

Christianity teaches that God is the sovereign Creator and Ruler of all. Christians believe in one God who exists in three eternal, coequal Persons—the Father, Son, and Holy Spirit (Trinity). God loves because his very nature is love. His divine mercy is an extension of his character. God is all-knowing and wants a relationship with people that is based on love and faith (Mark 12:30).

Christianity teaches a "***grace-based salvation***." A person is saved by God's grace (the undeserved blessing) through faith in Jesus Christ's death and resurrection. God, in His grace and mercy, has given His Son as the substitute for our sins. Colossians 1:13-14 says, *"When you were dead in your sins God made you alive with Christ. He forgave us all our sins, having canceled the charge of our legal indebtedness, which stood against us and condemned us; he has taken it away, nailing it to the cross."* The Bible shows how the death of the perfect Son of God was essential to pay for the sins of the world.

Islam teaches a **_works-based salvation_**, and in this way is much like other man-made religions. A Muslim must uphold the *Five Pillars of Islam.* He must confess the *Shahadah:* there is no God but Allah, and Muhammad is his prophet. He must kneel in prayer toward Mecca five times a day and must fast during the daylight hours one month of the year (*Ramadan*). He must give money to the poor and make a pilgrimage to Mecca sometime in his lifetime.

Islam teaches that the day of judgment will involve a person's good and bad deeds being weighed in a balance, so the standard for judgment is one's actions (*Surah 7:8-9, 21:47*). The Qur'an pointedly denies the death of Jesus (or Isa) on the cross (*Surah 3:55; 4:157-158*). To be saved, you must save yourself.

In Christianity, the **Antichrist** will be a charismatic political ruler who will rule during the 7 years known as the Tribulation. He will head a vast army and will be full of blasphemy. He will come from one of the gentile nations and will wage war on the people. Jesus will return to defeat the Antichrist and reign as King.

In Islam**, Al-Masih ad-Dajjal** is a prominent figure in Islamic end-time beliefs. *Masih* is an Arabic title applied to Jesus, roughly meaning *"messiah." Dajjal* means *"greatest lie"* or *"most deceitful."* Combined the phrase Al-Masih ad-Dajjal literally means *"the fraudulent Jesus"* or *"the lying Messiah."*

Often referred to as **Dajjal**, this character is the Muslim equivalent of the Antichrist in Christian eschatology. Muslims generally believe in the appearance of another end-of-times figure, known as the **Mahdi**, meaning "guided one." The Mahdi is considered a descendant of Muhammad who will appear shortly before the Prophet **Isa** (Jesus) and lead Muslims to rule the world.

You would think that both religions would somewhat agree on **Satan**, but that is not the case. In Christianity, Satan is a fallen angel who brought with him 1/3 of the angels of heaven in defiance of God. He's the source of evil and has ever been the tempter and accuser of humankind. The Book of Revelation states that Satan and his armies will be defeated and spend eternity in the Lake of Fire.

The Quran states that **Satan is Jinn** and not a fallen angel. Jinn are supernatural creatures created from a "smokeless and scorching fire," and can appear in human or animal form to interact with people. From the word jinn, we get our English word **genie**, defined as a spirit in human form who grants wishes. Jinn are often considered the Islamic equivalent of demons.

Islam, Judaism, and **Christianity** have different beliefs on essential doctrines such as God, Jesus, Scripture, and salvation. Christianity splits off from Judaism by the belief that **Jesus of Nazareth was the Messiah**, sent by God to redeem humanity. The Jewish religion **rejected Jesus** and said that they are still waiting for the Messiah. Islam says that **Jesus was one of the great prophets,** but not the savior of humanity. It expresses that Mohammed was the last of the great prophets, sent to clarify and complete God's message.

In closing, let's revisit Abraham, an important religious figure for Muslims, Christians, and Jews. Each religion uses Abraham in a specific way that would enhance their religious traditions.

In the Jewish religion, Abraham had a principal role, but his grandson Jacob was given the name Israel and was considered by many as the founder of the people of Israel. The apostle Paul wrote in the Book of Romans that Abraham was an example of Christian faith. Unlike those justified under the law given to Moses, Abraham, who lived before Moses and before the Law, was justified by his faith. God gave him a promise, Abraham believed in that promise, and his belief counted him as righteous. Christianity states that through faith in Jesus, ALL of Abraham's descendants may come into God's blessing of grace.

A comment from the Muslim side is that the first man God created was Adam, and he preached Islam, as did those after him, including Noah and Abraham. The third chapter of the Qur'an states that Abraham was a Muslim.

While Muslims somewhat respect the right of Christians to remain Christian, they believe that Christians would be better off if they converted to Islam. Christians could likewise say that Muslims would be better off if they converted to Christianity.

Most people follow the religion of their parents or culture, but I assure you that when each of us stands before God on Judgment Day, our eternity will be based on our believing in the true God. So, with so many religions, who is the true God?

Jesus easily answered that question for us. "I am the way and the truth and the life. No one comes to the Father except through me" (John 14:6).

So, the final question is: Does Abraham represent the Christian and Islamic religions? If you look at genetics, the answer is yes. **Ishmael** was Abram's firstborn son and is considered a patriarch of Islam based on legends that have developed around him and information in the Qur'an.

In the Christian world, **Isaac**, Abraham's second son, received God's blessings, which he then passed on to his son Jacob and all his children. God reaffirmed the covenant He had made with Abraham by saying that He would make Isaac's descendants as numerous as the stars and bless all the nations of the earth through them (Genesis 26:1-6).

Ishmael, seemingly the father of the Arab nation, was the son of Abram and Hagar, Sarai's maid. **God made His lasting covenant with Abraham, Sarah, and Isaac, not Abram, Hagar, and Ishmael.** Scripture shows that Ishmael was not a descendant of covenantal Abraham but of pre-covenantal Abram. Despite this, Muslims claim that Ishmael was a descendant of Abraham.

Muslims also reject the idea that God gave Canaan to Abraham's descendants as a gift, and that is why they refuse to accept modern Israel's right to exist. The promise that God would give Abraham and his descendants the land of Canaan is one of the major themes of the Pentateuch, the first five books of the Bible. God's gift of the land to Abraham contains three elements: a Promise, a Covenant, and an Oath.

But most importantly, the God who established a covenant with Abraham was also the God who sent His son Jesus to save people from their sinful nature and extend the Abraham covenant and eternal life to all who believe in Jesus Christ.

In the Islamic religion, there is no salvation through the blood of Christ because Jesus was merely a prophet. In Islam, there is no concept of salvation because life is just a "test" from Allah to see who will do the best. But genetics doesn't answer the burning question of how Islam can claim to be the correct and only religion if they do not believe in the Trinity or that Jesus (God's son) was the Messiah and died on the cross for all our sins.

So, how does God treat the Muslims in His New Heaven and New Earth plan? I don't know the answer to this question. However, I will offer this. While both religions may discuss the same topics, there is much disagreement between what is in the Quran and the Bible. Christians should always strive for good dialogue between the religions, but Christians should never water down their own beliefs to accommodate a theological common ground where there is none.

Moses warned the people of the danger of <u>false prophets</u> and said they should believe a special prophet that will arise from the Jews, and that person is the Lord Jesus Christ.

"The Lord said to me: "What they say is good. I will raise up for them a prophet like you from among their fellow Israelites, and I will put my words in his mouth. He will tell them everything I command him. I myself will call to account anyone who does not listen to my words that the prophet speaks in my name. But a prophet who presumes to speak in my name anything I have not commanded, or a prophet who speaks in the name of other gods, is to be put to death" (Deuteronomy 18:15-22, Acts 3:12-18).

If you look at all this information, Muhammad was not the prophet Moses or the counselor Jesus predicted. The message of Muhammad contradicts the message of Jesus and the Bible on many points. The only biblical prophecy that would apply to Muhammad would be:

"And many false prophets will appear and deceive many people..." (Matthew 24:11).

The core beliefs of Christian salvation revolve around the death, burial, and resurrection of Jesus, as well as his identity as a Savior and Ruler of the New Heavens and New Earth. Muslims don't believe in this at all.

Salvation: *"For God so loved the world, that he gave his only begotten Son, that whosoever believeth in him should not perish, but have everlasting life. For God sent not his Son into the world to condemn the world; but that the world through him might be saved. He that believeth on him is not condemned: but he that believeth not is condemned already, because he hath not believed in the name of the only begotten Son of God. And this is the condemnation, that light is come into the world, and men loved darkness rather than light,* *because their deeds were evil. For every one that doeth evil hateth the light, neither cometh to the light, lest his deeds should be reproved"* (John 3:16-20).

If you are looking for a strong and lasting link or relationship between Islam and Christianity, there is none. Jesus gave no room for any other Savior than himself.

Jesus offers a love so great that it surpasses knowledge. Love frees you from your sins, brings a special purpose to your life, and gives you the privilege of living an eternity with your Creator. Amen

Once Saved, Always Saved

If you, as a Christian, are challenged by someone saying that your salvation can be lost, how do you respond? Are you comfortable speaking the right words to express your true belief? It's a challenge that I don't think many of us are prepared to meet.

Let's suppose that Apostle Paul's life story was reversed. Suppose he spent the first part of his adult life preaching Christ's salvation, but the second part persecuting Christians. Would he be in Paradise today? Who in the Bible has sinned and stood condemned? Perhaps Adam and Eve, since God said that they would surely die if they ate of the tree of knowledge of good and evil.

Hebrews 6:4-8 is frequently cited by those who doubt the doctrine of eternal security more so than any other passage in the New Testament. For that reason, it can be said these words are among the New Testament's most misunderstood.

"It is impossible for those who have once been enlightened, who have tasted the heavenly gift, who have shared in the Holy Spirit, who have tasted the goodness of the word of God and the powers of the coming age and who have fallen away, to be brought back to repentance. To their loss they are

crucifying the Son of God all over again and subjecting him to public disgrace. Land that drinks in the rain often falling on it and that produces a crop useful to those for whom it is farmed receives the blessing of God. But land that produces thorns and thistles is worthless and is in danger of being cursed. In the end it will be burned."

But let's read on, starting at verse 9:

"But, beloved, we are persuaded better things of you, and things that accompany salvation, though we thus speak. For God is not unrighteous to forget your work and labour of love, which ye have shewed toward his name, in that ye have ministered to the saints, and do minister. And we desire that every one of you do shew the same diligence to the full assurance of hope unto the end: That ye be not slothful, but followers of them who through faith and patience inherit the promises."

When taken in context, Hebrews 6:4-8 warns Christians about the potential consequences of shallow, immature faith. Those who fall into doubt and disobedience cannot be "restored" except by the fire of God's judgment. There is a natural flow in this part of Hebrews: from spiritual immaturity to its consequences, to the confidence which should inspire our growth.

Chapter 6 expands on the dangers of shallow, immature faith. Rather than trying to re-explain the basics, the author intends to press on. According to this passage, shallow faith opens the risks of doubt, discouragement, and disobedience. These lead to a situation where one's only hope for restoration is through judgment, much as Israel experienced for forty years in the wilderness.

Since our hope is anchored in God's proven, unchanging, perfect, and absolute nature, we should be confident and patient rather than fearful. If you read closely, the purpose of the book of Hebrews is to warn against falling away and instruct how to avoid this. Children of God do sin, and there are conditions we must meet to be cleansed by Jesus' blood. *"To be cleansed by Jesus' blood, we must "walk in the light" and "confess our sins." To deny this is to deny the clear teaching of Scripture* (1 John 1:7-9).

"Repent of this wickedness and pray to the Lord in the hope that he may forgive you for having such a thought in your heart" (Acts 8:22).

So, does the Bible say that a child of God can sin and be lost? Christians feel that there is security in serving God faithfully. We should all try to overcome Satan's vengeance and ask forgiveness when sinning. But if we give our lives to Christ for a period and then fall away from our faith, do we still have a free pass to heaven? Of course, some will say that that person was never really saved. However, the scriptures state that you will have eternal life if you believe in Jesus Christ.

"He who has the Son has the life; he who does not have the Son of God does not have the life. These things I have written to you who believe in the name of the Son of God, so that you may know that you have eternal life" (1 John 5:12-13).

In a sermon by *Pastor David Jeremiah*, he recounted the true-life story of contemporaries *Billy Graham* and *Charles Templeton*. When both were young evangelists, many thought Templeton, rather than Graham, would achieve greater things in the name of the Lord. Both were good friends, but Templeton fell away from his Christian faith and declared himself to be an atheist. Most folks know Billy Graham's story, and how he turned out to be one of the world's most well-known evangelists. Before Templeton died in 2001 at the age of 86, he wrote a book titled *"Farewell to God."* In that book, Templeton talks about having a conversation with Graham. Templeton stated that he couldn't believe the biblical account of creation. Graham stated, "He believed the Genesis account of creation because it was in the Bible." Graham said, *"When I take the bible literally and proclaim it as the word of God, my preaching has power, and that is the path for me."*

Pastor Jeremiah shared the story of Graham and Templeton to remind his congregation that, as Christ followers, *"we are expected to run with endurance the race that has been set before us."* Yet, in his next breath, the pastor said that, while Templeton did not finish the race he started, he still has a place in God's kingdom. He said that it did not matter that Templeton renounced his Christian faith and said that he was an atheist because, since he had previously given his life to the Lord, he was secure for all eternity.

Once saved, always saved.

"I give them eternal life, and they shall never perish; no one will snatch them out of my hand. My Father, who has given them to me, is greater than all; no one can snatch them out of my Father's hand. I and the Father are one" (John 10:28–30).

"For I am convinced that neither death, nor life, nor angels, nor principalities, nor things present, nor things to come, nor powers, nor height, nor depth, nor any other created thing, will be able to separate us from the love of God, which is in Christ Jesus our Lord" (Romans 8:38–39).

So once a person is saved, they are saved forever. The entire book of Hebrews is addressed to Christians, and the wording of the following verse supports this:

"For it is by grace you have been saved, through faith— and this is not from yourselves, it is the gift of God, not by works, so that no one can boast" (Ephesians 2:8).

Too often, we argue and debate about many things in the Bible, but we need to remember that what we are reading are God's inspired words. The Bible is a product of divine inspiration. We believe Christ paid for all our sins—past, present, and future. Otherwise, we could not be redeemed. It would make no sense to say that Christ paid for "all" of a person's sins so he could be saved if ultimately the person is going to end up in Hell. The certificate of debt is canceled on the cross by your faith in Jesus. Works cannot lose salvation.

"If we confess our sins, he is faithful and just and will forgive us our sins and purify us from all unrighteousness" (1 John 1:9).

"Very truly I tell you, whoever hears my word and believes Him who sent me has eternal life and will not be judged" (John 5:24).

A person asks: I was baptized early and supposedly "saved." Over the years, I have fallen from grace and have done some evil things. What is my salvation status? When a sinner truly repents of their sins and believes in the Lord Jesus Christ as their personal Lord and Savior, they are justified before God and forgiven of their sins. You are "sealed" by the Holy Spirit, meaning you are a child of God. You cannot lose your salvation.

However, just because you believe in the statement "once saved, always saved" doesn't give you a license to sin. A person who says he has come to know Christ should not willingly go out and sin. Along with salvation, there is regeneration, which is the change in a person from being enslaved to sin to serving God. From being dead in his sins to alive in Christ. In John 3:3, this is what it means to be born again and to be made a new creature. We were buried with Christ through baptism into death so that, just as Christ was raised from the dead through the glory of the Father, we, too, may live a new life. Christians, like everyone else, struggle not to sin. The Holy Spirit helps in this ongoing war against sin.

The Book of Life or Lamb's Book of Life refers to eternal life by trusting in Jesus Christ (Rev 21:27). If you are in the Lamb's Book of Life, you have eternal life and will be in the eternal kingdom.

"The one who conquers will be clothed thus in white garments, and I will never blot his name out of the book of life. I will confess his name before my Father and before his angels" (Revelation 3:5).

Based on this verse, some believe names can be blotted out of the book, but that's not what it says. It says those who have trusted in Christ have their names in the Book of Life and will never be blotted out or erased. A person's name being in the Book of Life is vital as John wrote that *"if anyone's name was not found written in the Book of Life, he was thrown into the Lake of Fire"* (Revelation 20:15). The Book of the Living is thought to contain the names of those who are alive upon this earth (Psalms 69:28). It is constantly updated and revised as people are born and dying. Many scholars believe that the Book of Life and the Book of the Living are the same.

Jesus always does the will of the Father and does what is pleasing to the Father (John 8:29). He said it is the will of the Father that Jesus will not lose anyone. This demonstrates that once saved, always saved.

"My sheep hear My voice, and I know them, and they follow Me; and I give eternal life to them, and they shall never perish, and no one shall snatch them out of My hand" (John 10:27-28).

A true believer can never lose their salvation. They are eternally secure. It is dangerous when people say we can lose our salvation because it is close to saying that we have to work to keep our salvation. ***"If we could lose our eternal salvation, it wouldn't be eternal."*** Would God predestinate someone to be saved and then unsave them? I think not! God chose you. He will keep you and work in your life until the end to make you more like Christ.

> **"That everyone who believes may have eternal life in him. For God so loved the world that he gave his one and only Son, that whoever believes in him shall not perish but have eternal life"** (John 3:15-16).

> *"I assure you: Anyone who hears My word and believes Him who sent Me has eternal life and will not come under judgment but has passed from death to life"* (John 5:24).

> *"And we know that in all things God works for the good of those who love him, who have been called according to his purpose. For those God foreknew he also predestined to be conformed to the image of his Son, that he might be the firstborn among many brothers and sisters. And those he predestined, he also called; those he called, he also justified; those he justified, he also glorified"* (Romans 8:28-30).

> *"For he chose us in him before the creation of the world to be holy and blameless in his sight. In love he predestined us for adoption to sonship through Jesus Christ, in accordance with his pleasure and will"* (Ephesians 1:4).

Scripture shows that no one can take believers out of the Lord's hand or out of God's love in Jesus Christ. God saved you, and He will keep you! He promised us that He would.

> *"All those the Father gives me will come to me, and whoever comes to me I will never drive away. For I have come down from heaven not to do my will but to do the will of him who sent me. And this is the will of him who sent me, that I shall lose none of all those he has given me, but raise them up at the last day. For my Father's will is that everyone who looks*

to the Son and believes in him shall have eternal life, and I will raise them up at the last day" (John 6:37–40).

The Bible says that a Christian is "sealed" with the Holy Spirit <u>at the moment of their salvation</u> with the Lord and that nothing can break this seal, no matter how many nasty and evil sins a person may commit after getting saved.

Salvation is the gift of God, and God's gifts are irrevocable.
(Romans 11:29)

Credits

(*Sources used to develop these documents*)

The Bible (primarily the KJV)

Billy Graham literature

Dr. David Jeremiah literature

Pastor Mark Wilke

Scholar Gary Ray

GotQuestions

Unsealed.org

Wikipedia

Tim LaHaye and Thomas Ice

Phoenix Seminary

Baptist Standard

BibleStudyTools.com

Theology and Ministry

Basic internet searches

Randy Alcorn

Gene Nethery

Joe Johnston

www.ingramcontent.com/pod-product-compliance
Lightning Source LLC
Chambersburg PA
CBHW070549050426
42450CB00011B/2774